高级英汉互译
与学术交流

Advanced Academic Communication and Translation Between English and Chinese

许卉艳　姜桂桂
周英莉　杨晓华　编著

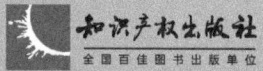

图书在版编目（CIP）数据

高级英汉互译与学术交流/许卉艳等编著. —北京：知识产权出版社，2019.1
ISBN 978-7-5130-6042-4

Ⅰ.①高… Ⅱ.①许… Ⅲ.①英语—翻译—教材 Ⅳ.①H315.9

中国版本图书馆CIP数据核字（2018）第297513号

内容提要

本书注重理论与实践相结合，练习设计符合学生学习逻辑，旨在培养其批判性思维能力和实践操作能力。

本书内容分为两大部分。1）英汉互译：介绍翻译的基本概念及英汉语言对比知识，结合实例解释各类翻译技巧和科技论文标题及摘要的翻译要领，并与之配套编写了适量的翻译实践和译文优化练习，给英语教与学提供了思维拓展空间。2）学术写作与交流：涉及学术论文写作以及组织口头学术报告的全过程，如标题、摘要、关键词、引言、文献综述、研究结果与讨论及结论等的写作要求及要领，如何开篇、介绍研究方法、呈现讨论结果、与听众互动以及制作/使用PPT的技巧和方法，并提供了大量可操作的实用句型模版。

责任编辑：陈晶晶　　　　　　　　　　责任校对：谷　洋
封面设计：李志伟　　　　　　　　　　责任印制：孙婷婷

高级英汉互译与学术交流

许卉艳　姜桂桂　周英莉　杨晓华　编著

出版发行：知识产权出版社 有限责任公司	网　　址：http://www.ipph.cn
社　　址：北京市海淀区气象路50号院	邮　　编：100081
责编电话：010-82000860转8391	责编邮箱：shiny-chjj@163.com
发行电话：010-82000860转8101/8102	发行传真：010-82000893/82005070/82000270
印　　刷：北京虎彩文化传播有限公司	经　　销：各大网上书店、新华书店及相关专业书店
开　　本：720mm×1000mm　1/16	印　　张：12
版　　次：2019年1月第1版	印　　次：2019年1月第1次印刷
字　　数：230千字	定　　价：49.00元
ISBN 978-7-5130-6042-4	

出版权专有　侵权必究
如有印装质量问题，本社负责调换。

Contents

Part I Translation Between English and Chinese

Unit 1 General Introduction to Translation 3

Unit 2 Comparison Between Chinese and English Language 10

Unit 3 Translation Skill (1) Amplification & Omission 16

Unit 4 Translation Skill (2) Conversion & Negation 26

Unit 5 Translation Skill (3) Rendering of Passive Voice 43

Unit 6 Translation Skill (4) Rendering of Attributive & Adverbial Clauses ... 51

Unit 7 Translation Skill (5) Rendering of Long Sentences 64

Unit 8 Translation of Scientific Papers 72

Advanced Academic Communication and Translation Between English and Chinese

Part II Academic Writing and Presentation

Unit 1 General Introduction to Academic Writing 89

Unit 2 Title, Author, Affiliation and Key Words 108

Unit 3 Abstract 117

Unit 4 Introduction 130

Unit 5 Literature Review 138

Unit 6 Result, Discussion and Conclusion 147

Unit 7 Preparing Oral Presentation 153

Bibliography 185

Part I

Translation Between English and Chinese

Unit 1 General Introduction to Translation

1.1 Origin of Translation: The Tower of Babel

According to the Old Testament, after the Flood the children of Noah had children, and their children had children. At that time, the whole earth was of one language, and of one speech. And it came to pass, as they journeyed from the east, that they found a plain in the land of Shinar, and they dwelt there. And they said one to another, Go to, let us make brick, and burn them thoroughly. And they had brick for stone, and slime had they for morter. And they said, Go to, let us build us a city and a tower, whose top may reach unto heaven; and let us make us a name, lest we be scattered abroad upon the face of the whole earth. And the Lord came down to see the city and the tower, which the children of men built. And the Lord said, Behold, the people is one, and they have all one language; and this they begin to do: and now nothing will be restrained from them, which they have imagined to do. Go to, let us go down, and there confound their language, that they may not understand one another's speech. So the Lord scattered them abroad from thence upon the face of all the earth: and they left off to build the city. Therefore is the name of it called Babel; because the Lord did there confound the language of all the earth: and from thence did the Lord scatter them abroad upon the face of all the earth (King James Version) .

Since then people speak different languages and live in different parts of the world. As a result, language becomes the first barrier for them to communicate with each other, and of course they can't build the tower and city. However, they have never stopped communicating and exchanging in language and culture, that is the role translation has played.

1.2 Nature and Scope of Translation

1) Three Meanings of Translation

* Translating: the process (to translate; the activity rather than the tangible object);

* A translation: the product of the process of translating (i.e. the translated text);

* Translation: the abstract concept which encompasses both the process of translating and the product of that process. (Roger T. Bell, 1995)

2) Definitions of Translation

* In a narrow sense, translation means to express the meaning of a certain text of a language by using another language, e.g. English-Chinese Translation/Chinese-English Translation (i.e. interlingual translation 语际翻译).

* In a broad sense, translation can also mean those kinds of translation between a dialect and the common language of a country, between one dialect and another dialect, between the old form and the modern form of a language, like the translation between classical Chinese and modern Chinese. It also includes the transformation between signs or numbers and a language. That is, intralingual translation (语内翻译) and intersemiotic translation (符际翻译).

* Translating consists in reproducing in the receptor language the closest natural equivalent of the source language message, first in terms of meaning, and second in terms of style. (Eugene A. Nida & Charles R. Taber, 1969)

* Translation is the expression in another language (or target language) of what has been expressed in another, source language, preserving semantic and stylistic equivalences. (Roger T. Bell, 1991)

* Translation is acculturation process between different cultures. (André Lefevere, 1992)

3) Definition of a Good Translation

Alexander F. Tytler [18th century British translation theorist, professor at the University of Edinburgh (1791)] described a good translation to be: that in which the merit of the original work is so completely transfused into another language, as to be as distinctly apprehended, and as strongly felt, by a native of the country to which that language belongs, as it is by those who speak the language of the original work.

4) Translator's Knowledge Bases and Skills

* Five knowledge bases: Source language (SL) knowledge, target language (TL) knowledge, text-type knowledge, domain knowledge and contrastive knowledge.

* Two skills: decoding + encoding

Translation: reading + writing

Interpretation: listening/reading + speaking

1.3 Principles or Criteria of Translation

1) Alexander Tytler (1790): Three Laws of Translation

* It should give a complete transcript of the ideas of the original work.

* The style and manner of writing should be of the same character with that of the original.

* The translation should have all the ease of original composition.

2) Yan Fu (1898): Triple Principle of "Xin, Da, Ya"

It means faithfulness/accuracy (full and complete conveying or transmission of the original content or thought), expressiveness/smoothness (the version must be clear and flowing without any grammatical mistakes or confused sense and logic), and elegance (the use of classical Chinese before the Han Dynasty).

According to Nida (2001), the three principles of faithfulness, expressiveness and elegance should be understood not as competitive but as additive factors: faithful equivalence in meaning, expressive clarity of form, and attractive elegance that makes a text a pleasure to read.

3) Two Commonly-Accepted Criteria

Faithfulness/accuracy and smoothness.

* Be faithful to the original content/meaning/views, original author's emotions and feelings, the original form and style.

* Be easy and readable rendering, forceful, clear and idiomatic expression in the target language, free from stiff formula and mechanical copying from dictionaries.

1.4 Translation Process

Translating is a complex and fascinating task. In fact, I. A. Richard (1953) has claimed that it is probably the most complex type of event in the history of cosmos.

The process of translation consists of three phases: comprehension, expression and check. Here we just focus on the first two stages.

1) Comprehension

As to comprehension, there are two famous sayings: You know a word by the company it keeps. No context, no text. Therefore, it is very necessary for translators to understand the word meaning through linguistic context and background knowledge.

Translate the following sentences:

(1) She cried her eyes out.

(2) The girl soon laid the table.

(3) His fury was exaggerated.

(4) From life to death is man's reach.

(5) Let any man come; I am his man.

(6) Theory is something but practice is everything.

(7) In learning English, grammar is not everything.

(8) I have read your articles. I expected to meet an older man.

2) Expression

In expression, there are two main methods: literal translation and free translation.

(1) Literal Translation

It means "not to alter the original words and sentences", but strives "to keep the sentiments and style of the original." For example:

crocodile's tears 鳄鱼的眼泪　　　　　armed to the teeth 武装到牙齿

to add fuel to the fire 火上加油　　　 to fish in troubled water 浑水摸鱼

a gentleman's agreement 君子协定　　 to break the record 打破纪录

(2) Free Translation

It is used mainly to convey the meaning and spirit of the original without trying to reproduce its sentence patterns or figures of speech, i.e."得意忘形".For example:

at sixes and sevens 乱七八糟　　　　　in two minds 三心二意

in threes and fours 三五成行　　　　　It rains cats and dogs. 大雨滂沱

Translate the following sentences or choose a better version:

(1) They parted enemies.

(2) Justice has long arms.

(3) Last night I heard him driving his pigs to market.

(4) The talk about raising taxes was a red flag to many voters.

(5) She knew I knew and she knew if she got funny I'd either ruin the romance or make her marry him, so she was very friendly.

　　(A) 她知道我知道她和他的事,她也明白她要是跟我过不去,破坏或成全他们全在我的一念之间,所以她对我很客气。

　　(B) 她很了解我,我很了解她;要是她遭遇困难,我得牺牲我们的浪漫,让她同他结婚,因为她待我太好了。

(3) Literal Translation and Free Translation

At the word or phrase level, we do have 100 percent literal translation or free translation, but at sentence level and beyond, it is quite common to see the combination of both literal translation and free translation. For example:

(1) Some officials often pay lip-service to education but don't work for better

schools.

一些官员们经常口惠而实不至，口口声声支持教育，却又不肯为改善学校条件做一些实际工作。

(2) The splitting of the atom was first used in warfare, but after Hiroshima and Nagasaki a grand effort began to provide electricity "too cheap to meter," freeing the world from its dependence on fossil fuels.

原子核裂变技术首先被用于战争，但是继广岛和长崎原子弹事件之后，这一伟大的发明便用来为人类提供"物美价廉"的电力，让世界摆脱对化石燃料的依赖。

1.5 Translation and Culture: Foreignization and Domestication

Translation and culture are inseparable. In fact, translation is a cross-lingual, cross-cultural and cross-social activity. "Domesticating translation" and "foreignizing translation" are two strategies coined by Lawrence Venuti (1995) to deal with cultural elements in translating. The former (target culture-oriented) refers to a transparent, fluent style is adopted in order to minimize the strangeness of the foreign text for target language readers, while the latter (source culture-oriented) designates the type of translation "deliberately breaks target conventions by retaining something of the foreignness of the original." The key difference between them is whether we keep the foreignness or not. The most famous representatives of each school are Nida and Venuti.

Let's look at the translation of "谋事在人，成事在天", which one is foreignization? Which one is domestication?

Man proposes, God disposes. (By David Hawkes)

Man proposes, Heaven disposes. (By Yang Xianyi)

Reflections and Practice

I. Discuss the following questions:

1. Is translation important or not? Any examples to support your idea?
2. What's your opinion on the principles or criteria of translation?

Ⅱ. Improve the following translations according to the original:

1. 相对于产品市场，要素市场改革一直相对滞后。

Relative to the product market, factor market reform has been relatively lagging behind.

2. 2015年我国天然气占一次能源消费的5.9%，远低于世界平均水平的23.8%。

Natural gas contributed to 5.9% of the primary energy consumption of China in 2015, which was 23.8% far lower than the world average level.

3. 这些意见涉及发改、财政、环保、住建、交通、工信、国土等众多强力部门。

These suggestions are related to the development and reform, finance, environmental protection, housing construction, transportation, public letter, land and many other powerful departments.

4. DC power supplies have a negative and positive terminal.

直流电源有消极终端和积极终端。

5. Forward-Looking Analysis on Obama Administration's China Policy and Countermeasures.

奥巴马政府的中国政策与对策的前瞻性分析。

6. We have good reason to think kindly of a school that has provided all our children with an excellent education.

对于为我们所有孩子提供了优质教育的学校，我们有很好的理由友好地看待它。

Unit 2 Comparison Between Chinese and English Language

2.1 Language Features

1) Analytic and Synthetic Language

Chinese is an analytic language with much fewer inflections: no fixed part of speech, no inflections in different tense, voice, mood of a verb. Phrases and sentences are formed according to word order and empty words. For example, the parts of speech of 学习, 政治, 困难 in "学习政治, 政治学习; 克服困难, 困难问题" are determined by their word order, context and logic. However, English language is both analytic and synthetic with rich inflections: flections in persona, tense, voice, mood, tone and non-predicate form (infinitive, participle) for a verb; single or plural form for a noun; comparative form for an adjective or an adverb. Phrases and sentences are formed according to word order and auxiliaries. Therefore, when rendering into Chinese, we need change the part of speech or add words to express different flections in English. For example:

(1) The things in the universe are changing all the time.

宇宙中的万物总是在不断变化的。

(2) Oxford has, or had till yesterday, fewer students than the University of Toronto.

无论现在还是过去, 牛津的在校学生数都比多伦多大学少得多。

2) Static and Dynamic Description

Static description is much often used in English, while dynamic description in

Chinese. As a result, English sentences overuse nouns, prepositions, adjectives and adverbs, while verbs, 4-character phrases and short sentences dominate Chinese. Therefore, it is quite natural to make some conversions in parts of speech and sentence structures in translation. For example:

(1) The computer is a far more careful and industrious inspector than human beings.

计算机比人检查得更仔细、更勤快。

(2) It is rather for us to be here dedicated to the great task remaining before us—that government of the people, by the people, for the people, shall not perish from the earth.

倒是我们应该在这里把自己奉献于仍然留在我们面前的伟大任务,以便使这个民有、民治、民享的政府永世长存。

(3) 正是由于他为人谦虚、体贴别人,他才赢得同事的尊重。

It is because he is modest and thoughtful that he is respected by his colleagues.

(4) 社会主义的主要目标是解放和发展生产力,消灭剥削,消除贫富两极分化,最终达到共同富裕。

The main goals of socialism are the liberation and development of productive forces, the elimination of exploitation, and polarization between the rich and the poor and the final achievement of common prosperity.

2.2 Word Order and Logical Order

1) Word Order

Each nation has its own unique ways to generate some idiomatic expressions, and English and Chinese are no exception.

track and field 田径　　　　　　　　　sooner or later 迟早
one and the same 同一的　　　　　　　one and only 唯一的
rain or shine 不论晴雨　　　　　　　　East China 华东
share the weal and woe 祸福与共
every means possible 一切可能的手段
back and forth, to and fro 前前后后,来来去去
suffer from cold and hunger 饥寒交迫

inconsistency of deeds with words 言行不一

food, clothing, shelter/housing and transportation 衣食住行

Besides, when more than one adjectives modify the noun in an English or a Chinese sentence, it usually follows a principle of either subjective → objective sequence or vice versa. For example:

a small round wooden table 一张木头小圆桌

the advanced foreign experience 外国的先进经验

国际先进水平 advanced international/world level

近代先进科学技术 advanced modern science and technology

全国性大规模的油气勘探 the large-scale national oil and gas exploration

2) Logical Order

Adverbial of cause, result, condition, supposition and purpose in English can be preceded or followed by the main clause, while in Chinese it usually follows the order: cause → result, condition → result, introduction → transition, action → purpose. For example:

积劳成疾 Fall ill through constant overwork

推陈出新 Evolve new things [the new] from the old

虽败犹荣 Lose gloriously/Glorious defeat

2.3 Sentence Structure

1) Loose vs. Periodic Sentence

An English sentence is just like a bunch of grapes with short stem (subject, verb or object) and lots of fruits (attributive and adverbials). That is to say, most of English sentences have loose structure with most important part at the beginning and least important in the end. A Chinese sentence is either like a bamboo or a dish of pearl and has periodic structure with most important part in the end. Therefore, it is quite common to see the conversion between loose and periodic structure in English and Chinese translation. For example:

Unit 2 Comparison Between Chinese and English Language

(1) It may seem strange that in this modern electronic time, the physicists are still a very long way from understanding the ultimate structure of matter or existence.

当今电子时代,物理学家们还远没有弄清物质/存在的最终结构,这似乎有些不可思议。

(2) Rocket research has confirmed a strange fact which had already been suspected there is a "high-temperature belt" in the atmosphere, with its center roughly thirty miles above the ground.

人们早就怀疑大气层中有一个高温带,其中心在距地面约30英里高的地方。利用火箭加以研究以后,这一奇异的事实已得到了证实。

(3) I am always amazed when I hear people saying that sport creates goodwill between the nations, and that if only the common peoples of the world could meet one another at football or cricket, they would have no inclination to meet on the battlefield.

每当我听人们说体育运动可建立国家之间的友谊,还说各国民众若在足球场或板球场上交锋,就不愿在战场上残杀的时候,我总是惊愕不已。

2) Parataxis vs. Hypotaxis

As some linguists suggest, English is more hypotactic（形合）, where syntactical relations are expressed by connectives; Chinese is more paratactic（意合）, in which clauses or phrases are placed one after another without coordinating connectives. Therefore, it is necessary for translators to convert from paratactic structure to hypotactic one or vice versa. For example:

(1) Action is equal to reaction, but it acts in a contrary direction.

作用力与反作用力大小相等,方向相反。

(2)（若）知己（又）知彼,（则）（虽）百战（而）不殆;（若）不知彼而知己,（则）（将）一胜（及）一负;（若）不知彼（又）不知己,（则）每战（将）必殆。

You can fight a hundred battles without defeat if you know the enemy as well as yourself. You will win one battle and lose one battle if you know yourself but are in the dark about the enemy. You will lose every battle if you are in the dark about both the enemy and yourself.

3) Passive Voice vs. Active Voice

Passive voice is widely used in English, especially in scientific literatures, but less commonly used in Chinese. Here let's look at an example to see how often the passive and active voice used in English and Chinese.

Vegetable oil has been known from antiquity. No household can get on without it, for it is used in cooking. Perfumes may be made from the oils of certain flowers. Soaps are made from vegetable and animal oils.

植物油自古以来就为人们所熟悉。任何家庭都离不开它,因为做饭的时候就要用它。有些花儿产生的油可以用来制造香水。植物油和动物油还可以用来制作肥皂。

In the above text, four passive voices are converted into three active and one passive in Chinese sentence.

Translation Practice:

I. Put the following paragraphs into Chinese/English:

1. For many people the need for human translators seems paradoxical in this age of computers. Since modern computer can be loaded with dictionaries and grammars, why not let computers do the work? Computers can perform certain very simple interlingual tasks, providing there is sufficient pre-editing and post-editing. But neither advertising brochures nor lyric poetry can ever be reduced to the kind of logic required of computer programs. Computer printouts of translations can often be understood, if the persons involved already know what the text is supposed to say. But the results of machine translating are usually in an unnatural form of language and sometimes just plain weird. Furthermore, real improvements will not come from merely doctoring the program or adding rules. The human brain is not only digital and analogical, but it also has a built-in system of values which gives it a componentially incalculable advantage over machines. Human translation will always be necessary for any text which is stylistically appealing and semantically complex, which includes most of what is worth communicating in another language. (Nida)

2. 翻译的意义是将词句从一种语言转换成另一种语言。简单地讲,它是用与原作不同的语言将作者的真正意思准确地复述出来的一种艺术。从以上翻译的定义来看,我们知道词句的原意必须尽可能保持准确,不可有所增删。翻译者的任务只是变换词汇而不是改变其意思。因此,翻译有两种要素:准确性与表达性。

II. Improve the following translations according to the original:

1. 很多工商业小锅炉和民用煤炉排放不达标。

Many industrial and commercial small boilers and civilian coal-fired stoves fail to meet the emission standard.

2. 我们应该学习借鉴国外先进技术,避免闭门造车。

We should learn from foreign advanced technologies and avoid divorcing ourselves from the masses and from reality and act blindly.

3. 天然气发展潜力巨大。未来天然气消费空间广阔。

The development of natural gas has a huge potential. The consumption space of natural gas has a bright prospect.

4. A converse effect is the cooling of a gas when it expands.

一种逆效应是气体在膨胀时将其冷却。

5. The total investment in solar for the next year would be remarkable considering that capital costs for solar technology continue to fall sharply.

明年太阳能投资额有可能非常可观,考虑到当前太阳能技术的资本成本持续大幅下降。

6. The developed countries are rich in skilled work force and capital resources, so they can concentrate on producing many technology-intensive products such as computers, aircrafts, and so on.

发达国家在熟练劳动力和资本方面富有,所以它们能集中生产很多技术密集型的产品,比如计算机、飞机等。

Unit 3 Translation Skill (1) Amplification & Omission

3.1 Amplification in English-Chinese Translation

Amplification, also called addition, means supplying necessary words in the translation on the basis of accurate comprehension of the original.

1) Adding Words to Make an Abstract Concept Clear

derivation 推导过程   solution 解决方法
evolution 进化过程   jealousy 嫉妒心理
best-sellerdom 畅销圈子   backwardness 落后状态

(1) His uneasy cheerfulness was painful to watch.

他那高兴而不安的神情，叫人看起来就感到痛心。

(2) When the exploration was completed, the two astronauts on the moon would join the moon-ship once more.

完成勘查工作之后，登上月球的两个宇航员将重新回到船舱内。

2) Adding Words to Indicate Plural Nouns

There is no change of forms for Chinese plural nouns, while English nouns have but with few quantity words. Therefore, in English-Chinese translation, we have to add words like overlapping words, numerals, words of generalization, and adverbs etc. to express the concept of plural.

(1) These hospital expenses made inroads on their savings.

这些住院费严重地消耗了他们的积蓄。

(2) Note that the words "velocity" and "speed" require explanation.

请注意,"速度"和"速率"这两个词需要解释。

(3) Professional schools began to be founded as the demand for engineers steadily increased in the 1950s.

20世纪50年代由于对工程师的需求不断增加,人们开始建立一批批的职业学校。

(4) Governments and businesses together with the United Nations are mobilizing efforts to achieve the Sustainable Development Agenda by 2030.

各国政府、企业与联合国携手,正在为到2030年实现"可持续发展议程"而尽心竭力。

3) Adding Omitted Words to Convey the Original Meaning

(1) Matter can be changed into energy and energy into matter.

物质可以转化为能,能也可以转化为物质。

(2) Ice is the solid state; water the liquid state, and water vapor the gaseous state.

冰是固态,水是液态,水蒸气是气态。

(3) Reading exercises one's eyes; speaking, one's tongue; while writing, one's mind.

阅读训练人的眼睛,说话训练人的口齿,写作训练人的思维。

4) Adding Words to Express Different Tenses

Auxiliary verbs (will, be, have) are used in English to express the different tenses, but in Chinese we have to resort to some words, such as "曾、曾经、已(经)、过、了"(for perfect tense);"正(在)、在、着……"(for progressive tense);"将、要、会、就、便、了"(for future tense);"过去、以前、曾(经)、当时"(for past tense);"现在、目前"(for present tense);"一直、一向"(for continuous perfect tense)。

(1) I was, and remain, grateful for the part he played in my success.

我的成功有他的功劳,对此我过去很感激,现在仍很感激。

(2) Without quantum theory of Einstein there would never have been any practical utilization of nuclear power.

要是没有爱因斯坦的量子论,永远也不会有核能的实际应用。

(3) We will continue to improve the consumption proportion of clean energy like natural gas and non-fossil energy, and strive to create green GDP.

我们要不断地提高天然气、非化石能源等清洁能源的消费比重,努力创造绿色GDP。

5) Adding Necessary Connectives

(1) His reputation and achievements outlive him.

虽然他已经去世,可是他的名声和成就依然存在。

(2) Heat from the sun stirs up the atmosphere, generating wind.

太阳发出的热能搅动大气,于是产生了风。

(3) The best lubricant cannot maintain oil films between the surfaces of engineering gears.

即使是最好的润滑油,在啮合处也不能保住油膜。

6) Adding Classifiers

In English there is only "a/an/the" or "a piece of", etc. to modify the single noun, while in Chinese, different nouns require the use of different classifiers, such as "一堆、一只、一个、一件、一张、一颗、一块、一副、一根、一辆、一轮、一位、一台、一扇、一本、一行、一种、一方、一项". And even some classifiers are used to express a certain action, for example, "停一下、休息一下、吵了一顿", etc.

(1) He gave her a gentle push.

他轻轻地推了她一下。

(2) A stream was winding its way through the valley into the river.

一弯溪水蜿蜒流过山谷,汇入江里去了。

(3) He made a speech, eloquently advocating his company of the future.

他发表了一通言论,振振有词地把他未来的公司鼓吹一番。

3.2 Amplification in Chinese-English Translation

They are mainly used in the following cases:

1) Adding Necessary Connectives

（1）汽油贵得惊人，我们就很少用车。

Because of fantastically high price of gasoline, we seldom used our car.

（2）正确的选择可以造就生命中灿烂的前程，错误的选择可以毁掉生活的梦想。

A right choice can bring us a brighter future, but a wrong one may ruin our dreams toward life.

（3）在能源资源战略属性日益突出的情况下，一味追求控股往往脱离实际，并且可能要付出很高的经济和政治代价，似应予以淡化。

In the context of increasingly prominent strategic attributes of energy resources, it seems that a blind pursuit of holdings should be played down due to its frequent divorce from reality, and possibly high economic and political costs.

2) Adding Necessary Pronouns

（1）必须勤学苦练，才能精通一门外国语。

One must study hard before mastering a foreign language.

（2）交出译文之前，必须读几遍，看看有没有要修改的地方。

Before handing in your translation, you have to read it over and over again and see if there is anything in it to be corrected or improved.

（3）忽视科技的创造性、智能性特点，则管理无功且损害科技事业。

If we ignore the creativity and intelligence of technology, we will do no good to management and even do damage to sci-tech undertakings.

Translation Practice 1:

I. Put the following sentences into Chinese/English:

1. Decisiveness, perseverance, flexibility are keys for people to succeed in business.

2. Were there no electric pressure in a conductor, the electron flow would not take place in it.

3. The major problem in fabrication is the control of contamination and foreign

materials, e.g. that of drugs.

4. I was extremely worried about her, but this was neither the place nor the time for a lecture or an argument.

5. The real reason why prices were, and still are, too high is complicated, no short discussion can satisfactorily explain this problem.

6. He was equally at home with the abstractions of number theory, the long calculations of astronomy and the practicalities of applied physics.

7. 他通宵没睡，眼睛都熬红了。

8. 喝了几杯酒，他脸上红扑扑的。

9. 三十年代他红得发紫，战后就默默无闻了。

10. 要改变这个厂的经济状况得花大力气。

11. 白猫、黑猫，逮到耗子就是好猫。

12. 面对困难，坚定信心，依靠科技进步助推煤层气产业。

Ⅱ. Improve the following translations according to the original:

1. 没有调查就没有发言权。

There is no investigation and study and no right to speak.

2. 中国天然气取得了飞跃式发展。

The natural gas has made leap-forward development in China.

3. 这本畅销书对读者产生了巨大的影响。

The bestseller had a great impact on readers.

4. Gas, oil, and electric furnaces are most commonly used for heat treating metal.

煤气、石油和电炉最常用来热处理金属。

5. You must know the properties of the instrument before you use it.

使用仪器前，必须弄清它的性能。

6. It is necessary to establish a voluntary carbon market or an emission trading scheme to ensure emission compliance of businesses.

有必要建立一个自觉自愿的碳市场或一种排放交易计划，以保证企业对排放的服从。

Unit 3 Translation Skill (1) Amplification & Omission

3.3 Omission in English-Chinese Translation

Generally speaking, omission in English-Chinese translation is used to achieve succinctness, especially in dealing with excessive use of English pronouns and English function words such as the article, preposition, conjunction, etc.

1) Omission of Personal Pronouns and Possessive Pronouns

Pronouns are much more frequently used in English than in Chinese. When translated into Chinese, many of them may be omitted so as to make the rendering conform to Chinese usage.

(1) If you give him an inch, he will take a mile.

得寸进尺。

(2) He put his hands into his pockets and then shrugged his shoulders.

他将双手放进衣袋，然后耸了耸肩。

(3) They went into dinner. It was excellent, and the wine was good. Its influence presently had its effect on them. They talked not only without acrimony, but even with friendliness. (Maugham)

他们进入餐室用餐。美酒佳肴，顿受感染，言谈间不但没有恶言恶语，甚至还充满友好之情。

2) Omission of Impersonal Pronoun "It"

This case often occurs when "it" refers to something indefinite or meaningless.

(1) It was Pasteur who discovered that diseases are caused by living germs.

是巴斯德发现了疾病是由活着的病菌引起的。

(2) Let's make it 4 o'clock on Friday afternoon to have a talk in my office.

就让我们定在周五下午四点在我办公室谈吧。

(3) It was not until the 19th century that heat was considered as a form of energy.

直到19世纪人们才认识到热是能量的一种形式。

3) Omission of Conjunctions

(1) Like charges repel each other while opposite charges attract.

同性电荷相斥,异性电荷相吸。

(2) Practically all substances expand when heated and contract when cooled.

几乎所有的物质都热胀冷缩。

(3) Never get on or off the bus before it comes to a standstill.

车未停稳,请勿上下车。

4) Omission of Articles

(1) Birds of a feather flock together.

物以类聚,人以群分。

(2) Any substance is made of atoms whether it is a solid, a liquid, or a gas.

任何物质,不论是固体、液体还是气体,都由原子组成。

Note: Articles can't be omitted when they mean "一""每一""某一", or something important. For example:

(3) Take the medicine three times a day. 每天服药三次。

5) Omission of Prepositions

(1) Smoking in public places is prohibited.

公共场所禁止吸烟。

(2) Hydrogen is the lightest element with an atomic weight of 1.0008.

氢是最轻的元素,原子量为1.0008。

(3) The products produced by this factory are good in quality and low in price.

该厂生产的产品物美价廉。

6) Omission of Verbs

(1) When the pressure gets low, the boiling-point becomes low.

气压低,沸点就低。

(2) These developing countries cover vast territories, encompass a large population and abound in natural resources.

这些发展中国家地大物博,人口众多。

3.4 Omission in Chinese-English Translation

The technique of omission can also be used in Chinese-English translation, mostly in the following cases:

1) Omitting Unnecessary Repetition

（1）中央要发展工业，地方也要发展工业。

The central authorities want to develop industry, and so do the local authorities.

（2）我曾经遇到过，不是氧气设备出故障，就是引擎出故障，或两者都出故障。

I had experienced oxygen and/or engine trouble.

（3）一个地方有一个地方的全局，一个国家有一个国家的全局，全世界有全世界的全局。

A locality has its own over-all interests; a nation has another and the earth yet another.

2) Omitting Classifiers and Numerals of Generalization

（1）电流的主要效应有磁效应、热效应和化学效应三种。

The chief effects of electric currents are the magnetic, heating, and chemical effects.

（2）刑事案件中以精神错乱为由进行辩护，这是一个涉及医学、法律和道德三方面的问题。

The issue of insanity as a defense in criminal cases is at the interface of medicine, law and ethics.

3) Omitting Abstract Category Nouns

Sometimes some nouns like 任务、工作、情况、问题、事业、局面、现象、性质 and the like do not indicate a specific notion but an abstract concept, so omission is used here. For example:

（1）希望中东地区的人民早日结束社会动荡和纷扰不安的局面。

It is hoped that people in the Middle East areas can put an early end to the social unrest and upheaval.

（2）她的朋友们听到她家中的困难情况后，都主动伸出援助之手。

After her friends heard about her family difficulties, they offered her a helping hand.

（3）为了办好2008年北京奥运会，中国政府和人民做了大量的准备工作。

Chinese government and people have done a lot of preparations to ensure the success of the 2008 Beijing Olympic Games.

Translation Practice 2:

I. Put the following sentences into Chinese/English:

1. Thermoplastic plastics become soft if they are heated.

2. He shrugged his shoulders, shook his head, cast up his eyes, but said nothing.

3. University applicants who had worked at a job would receive preference over those who had not.

4. The new computer is easy to operate, versatile, compact and has a pleasing modern design.

5. Scientific exploration, the search for knowledge has given man the practical result of being able to shield himself from the calamities of nature and the calamities imposed by other man.

6. 21世纪我们应该大力发展教育和科技事业。

7. 党和政府要依靠社会各方面的力量，加大对中西部地区的支持力度。

8. 总之，就全国范围来说，我们一定能够逐步顺利解决沿海同内地贫富差距的问题。

9. 大城市应该积极推进住房体制改革，加快建立城市贫困居民的最低生活保障制度。

10. 这种新药缩短了病人康复的时间，减轻了他的病痛，也减少了可能出现的严重副作用。

II. Improve the following translations according to the original:

1. 电压、电流和电阻这三个因素是相互关联的。

The three factors, voltages, current and resistance, are related to each other.

2. 我们要加大政策支持力度，助力储气库快速建设。

We should increase policy supportive strength to assist the construction of gas storage.

3. 经过5600多次的试验，他们终于在2016年解决了这个技术难题。

After more than 5600 times of experiments, finally they solved this technical difficulty in 2016.

4. The output power of a machine is always smaller than its input power.

一台机器的输出功率总是小于其输入功率。

5. The waste gases are harmful to us and we should by all means remove them.

废气对我们是有害的,所以我们要尽力排除它们。

6. The film showed some big national park with government airplanes dropping food down to the deer when they got snowed and had nothing to eat.

电影演的是在某个大的国家公园,政府派飞机给那里的鹿扔食物,因为它们让雪给封住了,而且没吃的。

Unit 4 Translation Skill (2) Conversion & Negation

Conversion here refers to the change of parts of speech, of sentence elements and structures in translation.

4.1 Conversion

4.1.1 Conversion of Part of Speech

1) Conversion of Verbs

Since English is a static language and Chinese a dynamic one, so it is very common to see many different parts of speech in English are translated into Chinese verbs, and Chinese verbs into nouns, prepositions, adjectives or adverbs.

Noun ⟷ Verb

(1) The improvement of energy efficiency in a restaurant will not only save money, but also protect valuable natural resources.

提高餐厅的能源效率不仅能省钱，还能保护宝贵的自然资源。

(2) 大多数细菌不仅对人类无害，而且对延续地球上一切生命都是绝对必要的。

Most bacteria are not only harmless to man but are absolutely essential to the continuation of all life on earth.

Preposition ⟷ Verb

(1) Ammonia is a colorless gas with a very pungent odor.

氨是一种具有强烈刺激气味的无色气体。

(2) 即使用倍数最大的显微镜，也没有任何人看到过单个的原子或分子。

No one has ever seen a single atom or molecule even with the most powerful microscope.

Adjective ↔ Verb

Many English adjectives used after a link verb to indicate one's consciousness, feelings, emotions, desires, etc., are always converted into Chinese verbs. These words include: confident, certain, careful, cautious, angry, sure, ignorant, afraid, doubtful, aware, concerned, glad, delighted, sorry, ashamed, thankful, anxious, grateful, able and so on. It is just opposite in Chinese-English translation.

(1) A solar cell is reproductive by itself under any circumstances.

太阳能电池在任何情况下都可以自行充电。

(2) I am aware that Congress has passed the legislation on improving energy efficiency.

我知道议会已经通过了有关提高能源效率的立法。

(3) 他们既不向往功名利禄，也不一味追求物质享受。

They are not anxious social climbers, and they have no devotion to material things.

(4) 研究人员确信能研制出新的生产技术来提高煤炭的洁净利用率。

Researchers are confident that they can develop a new technique to enhance the clean utilization of coal.

Adverb ↔ Verb

(1) I like Fridays off.

我喜欢每周五休息。

(2) 没有人知道他要离开北京多久。

Nobody knows how long he will be away from Beijing.

2) Conversion of Nouns

Verb ↔ Noun

(1) These materials are characterized by good insulation and high resistance to wear.

这些材料的特点是：绝缘性好，耐磨性强。

(2) 该设计的目的在于操作自动化，调节方便，维护简易，生产率高。

The design aims at automatic operation, easy regulation, simple maintenance and high productivity.

Adjective ⟷ Noun

English adjectives with definite articles to indicate categories of people, things, or adjectives used as predicative to indicate the nature of things may also be converted into nouns.

(1) It is a fact that glass is much more soluble than quarts.

事实上,玻璃的可溶性比石英大得多。

(2) Both the compounds are acids; the former is strong, the latter weak.

这两种化合物都是酸,前者是强酸,后者是弱酸。

(3) 刀具必须有足够的强度、韧性、硬度,而且要耐磨。

The cutting tools must be strong, tough, hard, and wear resistant.

Adverb ⟷ Noun

(1) Human translation will always be necessary for any text which is stylistically appealing and semantically complex.

对于任何文体引人入胜、语义复杂的文本,非得由人工翻译不可。

(2) 调查表明,估计该地区拥有资源总量为 300 万吨。

The investigation shows that totally 3,000,000 tons of resources have been calculated.

Pronoun ⟷ Noun

(1) The specific resistance of iron is not so small as that of copper.

铁的电阻系数不如铜的电阻系数那样小。

(2) 重量的单位是克,长度的单位是米,容积的单位是升。

The unit of weight is the gram, that of length is the meter, and that of capacity is the liter.

3) Conversion of Adjectives

Noun ⟷ Adjective

(1) Speed and reliability are the chief advantage of the electronic computer.

高效、可靠是电子计算机的主要优点。

(2) 地球上的生命依赖水而生存,而水是不可替代的。

Life on earth depends on water, and there is no substitute for it.

<u>Adverb ⟷ Adjective</u>

(1) Earthquakes are closely related to faulting.

地震与断裂运动有密切的关系。

(2) 电子计算机的主要特点是计算准确而迅速。

The electronic computer is chiefly characterized by its accurate and quick computations.

4) Conversion of Adverbs

<u>Adjective ⟷ Adverb</u>

(1) We place the highest value on our friendly relationship with developing countries.

我们高度珍视同发展中国家的友好关系。

(2) 水在4℃以下就不断地膨胀而不是不断地收缩。

Below 4℃, water is in continuous expansion instead of continuous contraction.

<u>Noun ⟷ Adverb</u>

(1) I have the honor to inform you that your application has been accepted.

我荣幸地通知阁下，您的申请已被接受。

(2) 美国对日本慢吞吞地推进自由贸易进程感到不满。

The United States was unhappy with the slowness of Japan to advance free trade.

<u>Verb ⟷ Adverb</u>

(1) Rapid evaporation at the heating-surface tends to make the steam wet.

加热面上的迅速蒸发，往往使蒸汽的湿度变大。

(2) 林则徐认为，要成功地制止鸦片买卖，就得首先把鸦片焚毁。

Lin Zexu believed that a successful ban of the trade in opium must be preceded by the destruction of the drug itself.

4.1.2 Conversion of Sentence Elements

Sometimes, conversion also involves the change of various elements of a sentence, such as from the subject to the object, and vice versa. For example:

1) Conversion of the Subject

Subject ⟷ Predicate

(1) Much discussion today is about how to keep down the housing prices.

如今人们经常议论如何降低房价的问题。

(2) 应当始终注意保护计算机,使其免受各种病毒袭击。

Care must be taken at all times to protect the computer from viruses.

Subject ⟷ Object

(1) A stone given a push along a rough road is quickly stopped by friction.

如果在粗糙路面上推一下石头,石头就会因摩擦而很快停止运动。

(2) 利用发电机可以把机械能再转变成电能。

The mechanical energy can be changed back into electrical energy by means of a generator.

Subject ⟷ Adverbial

(1) Primary and secondary schools will impart to us only some rudiments of knowledge.

从小学到中学,我们所修习的无非是一些基本知识。

(2) 由于页岩气储量丰富,天然气价格一直处于低位。

Abundant shale gas reserves have helped to keep natural gas prices low.

Subject ⟷ Attributive

(1) A semi-conductor has a poor conductivity at room temperature, but it may become a good conductor at high temperature.

在室温下,半导体的电导率差,但在高温下,却可能成为良导体。

(2) 各种材料的磁特性差别很大。

Various substances differ widely in their magnetic characteristics.

2) Conversion of the Predicate

Predicate ⟷ Subject

(1) A "triangle" is defined as a plane figure with three sides and three angles.

"三角形"的定义是有3条边和3个角的平面图形。

(2) 气体和固体的区别在于气体比固体压缩性更强。

Unit 4 Translation Skill (2) Conversion & Negation

Gases differ from solids in that the former have greater compressibility than the latter.

3) Conversion of the Object

Object ↔ Subject

(1) An automobile must have a brake with high efficiency.

汽车的刹车必须高度有效。

(2) 水的密度是每立方英尺62.4磅。

Water has a density of 62.4 pounds per cubic foot.

Object ↔ Predicate

(1) The secretary cast impatient glances at the young man, turned away without answering his question.

秘书不耐烦地看了看这个年轻人,转过头去,没有回答他的问题。

(2) 尽管我们失败过,但仍要坚持下去。

We will preserve regardless of past failure.

4) Conversion of the Adverbial

Adverbial ↔ Subject

(1) Nearly 70 supporting projects for services have been completed in Shanghai's Qingpu District where the venue is located.

会展中心所在地上海市青浦区已完成了70多项支持性服务项目。

(2) The 20th century witnessed unparalleled growth in knowledge, wealth and health of human being.

在20世纪,人类的知识、财富以及健康等各方面都发生了前所未有的增长和改善。

Adverbial ↔ Attributive

(1) Tensions over trade are heating up between the United States and China.

中美之间的贸易关系变得越来越紧张。

(2) 一线城市如北京、上海、广州的房地产特别昂贵。

The real estate is very expensive in first-tier cities like Beijing, Shanghai and Guangzhou.

5) Conversion of the Attributive

Attributive ⟷ Predicate

(1) There is a large amount of energy wasted due to friction.

摩擦消耗了大量的能量。

(2) 某些金属具有导电能力。

There are some metals which possess the power to conduct electricity.

Attributive ⟷ Predicative

(1) The earth was formed from the same kind of material that makes up the sun.

构成地球的物质与构成太阳的物质是相同的。

(2) 解决雾霾天气问题的确是非常紧迫的。

To cope with hazy weather is indeed a most pressing problem.

Attributive ⟷ Adverbial

(1) We should have a firm grasp of the fundamentals of computer science.

我们应该牢固地掌握计算机基础知识。

(2) 本书生动地再现了大庆石油会战的情景。

The book presents a vivid picture of Oil Battle in Daqing Oilfield.

4.1.3 Conversion of Sentence Structure

In translation, it is difficult to get rid of the influence of the source language structure. Thus, some changes of the sentence structures should be made as the followings.

Simple Sentence ⟷ Compound or Complex Sentence

(1) Further delay would cause us greater losses.

我们如果再耽搁,将会蒙受更大的损失。

(2) With a solid educational foundation we can reap a lifetime of benefits.

学问要有根底,根底要打得坚实,以后将终生受用。

(3) 只要小心谨慎,骑摩托车并不像一般人所想象得那样危险。

Careful cyclists are in less danger than is commonly believed.

(4) 近年来,中美两国国民经济发展迅速,为两国的经济、贸易合作提供了良好的基础。

The rapid development of the national economies of China and the U.S. in recent years has laid a sound foundation for economic and trade cooperation between the two countries.

Compound or Complex Sentence → Simple Sentence

(1) Inside pressure rises when temperature rises.

内部的压力随着气温的升高而升高。

(2) A compound is a substance which is composed of the atoms of two or more different elements.

化合物这种物质是由两种或更多种不同元素的原子构成的。

(3) 由于该支护方法的机理尚不明确，桩板墙防护存在很多危险。

There are many risks in construction of the sheet-pile retaining wall due to complex reinforcement mechanism of anchors between piles.

(4) 人们通常都反对使用血管扩张剂，可是并不反对使用氨茶碱。

Aminophyllinge does not share the usual objection to vasodilators.

Sentence with Subject ↔ Sentences without Subject

(1) A little more care would have prevented such an accident.

如果当时稍加小心，就不会发生这次事故了。

(2) The pricing and subsidy mode for wind and photovoltaic power generation is still a controversy because it lacks the market competition mechanism to encourage technological advance.

对于风电、光伏发电的定价补贴模式一直存在争议，这种模式缺乏鼓励技术进步的市场竞争机制。

(3) 全盘否定过去能源和电力体制改革的言论有失偏颇，不符合实际。

It is biased and unrealistic to negate the past energy and power reform.

(4) 加快天然气储气库建设，同时鼓励发展企业商业储备，有助于提高储气规模和应急调峰能力。

It will help to expand reserve scale and emergency peak shaving ability to accelerate the construction of natural gas storage tank while encouraging the development of commercial reserves in enterprises.

Translation Practice 1:

I. Translate the following sentences, using the techniques of conversion:

1. We are enemies of all wars, but above all of nuclear wars.

2. The volume of trade has increased tremendously to the advantage of both China and Russia.

3. In the 1880s the United States was a land sharply divided between the immensely wealthy and the very poor.

4. My reflection when I first made myself master of the central idea of the Origin was "How extremely stupid not to have thought of that!"

5. The Asia-Pacific region is characterized by a diversity of economic, social and political systems, cultural traditions and values, languages and aspirations.

6. The target to attack standard tests is wrong, for in attacking the tests, critics divert attention from the fault that lies with ill-informed or incompetent users.

7. 科学家们深信,所有物质都是不灭的。

8. 本文的目的在于讨论原材料和技术的新成就。

9. 为了证实镭这种神秘物质,居里夫妇付出了辛勤的劳动。

10. 今天,信息时代已经取代了工业时代,并缩短了时间和距离。

11. 一位成功的科学家应善于观察、务求准确、具有耐心、客观求实。

12. 再深入研究产能改革和转型的关键推动力,我们会发现新趋势将会引领全球未来的炼油行业的走向。

II. Improve the following translations according to the original:

1. 如果没有钢铁,工业的发展就会寸步难行。

If there are no iron and steel, the development of industry would undergo extreme difficulties.

2. 实验结果表明了该方法的实用性和有效性。

Results of the experiments show the practicality and effectiveness of the proposed method.

3. 同期，科学数据的收集与分析表明北京的空气质量得到大大改善。

Over the same period, scientific data collection and analysis show that Beijing's air quality has made a great improvement.

4. People's tendency to be untruthful was greater in the afternoon than in the morning, the researchers found.

研究人员发现，人们不诚实的倾向下午比上午强。

5. Tesla is operating at a 55 to 60 per cent cost disadvantage compared to Chinese producers due to tariffs and shipping costs.

与中国生产商相比，由于关税和运输成本，特斯拉以55%~60%的劣势经营着。

6. India has made a progress in reforming market to improve availability of liquefied clean burning fuels in urban and rural area.

印度在改革市场、加强城市和乡村地区的液化清洁燃料的获取方面取得了进步。

4.2 Negation

As some linguists have pointed out, every language has its peculiarities in negation. And there are significant, though often neglected, differences between English and Chinese in negation—both in the way of thinking and in the mode of speaking.

For example, it is idiomatic to say "我认为他不对""我想他不会接受邀请" in Chinese. In English, however, the same ideas would be expressed as "I don't think he is correct", "I don't think he will accept the invitation", with the negative shifted to the beginning of the sentence.

English negative words and expressions mainly fall into the following categories:

* Full negatives: no, not, none, never, nothing, nobody, nowhere, neither, nor, etc.

* Semi negatives: hardly, scarcely, seldom, barely, few, little, etc.

* Partial negatives: not every, not all, not both, not much, not many, not always, etc.

* Words with negative implication: fail, without, beyond, until, unless, lest,

ignorant, refrain, refuse, neglect, absence, instead of, other than, except (for), rather than, more than, anything but, prefer... to, etc.

When translated into Chinese, these negative words and expressions should be adapted to idiomatic Chinese expressions.

4.2.1 Negation in English-Chinese Translation

1) Affirmative in English, Negative in Chinese.

Such cases are found in a wide range of expressions, words of different parts of speech, various phrases, or sentence structures.

(1) Your temper is more than I can bear. (conj.)

我受不了你的脾气。

(2) If it worked once, it can work twice. (sentence)

一次得手,再次不愁。

(3) It was beyond his power to sign such a contract. (prep.)

他无权签订这样的合同。

(4) The days passed quickly, but she worked as hard as ever. (adv.)

日子很快过去了,她做工作却丝毫没有放松。

(5) You've got to believe in yourself, even when no one else does. (verb)

即使没人相信你了,你也不能对自己绝望。

(6) We cannot finish the work in the absence of these conditions. (noun)

在不具备这些条件的情况下,我们不能完成这项工作。

(7) We believe that the younger generation will prove worthy of our trust. (phrase)

我们相信,年青一代将不会辜负我们的信任。

(8) The next species of intelligent life on the earth will be a creature like ourselves but with a very large head and weak muscles. (adj.)

地球上下一代智能生命将是类似于我们人类的一种动物:头颅硕大,肌肉不发达。

2) Negative in English, Affirmative in Chinese

This is just opposite to the previous cases.

Unit 4 Translation Skill (2) Conversion & Negation

(1) The machine has two serious disadvantages. (noun)

那台机器有两个严重缺陷。

(2) He is old, none the less he works like a young man. (phrase)

他虽然上了年纪,但干起活来,还像个年轻人。

(3) All the articles are untouchable in the museum. (adj.)

博物馆内的一切展品禁止触摸。

(4) Such flight couldn't long escape notice. (verb)

这类飞行迟早会被人发觉。

(5) No one but a great philosopher could solve such a question. (conj.)

只有大思想家才能解决这样的问题。

(6) Many agreed that the Prime Minister had in effect resigned dishonorably. (adv.)

许多人认为首相辞职实际上是很丢面子的。

(7) The spokesman deliberately refrained from expressing his opinion on the issue. (verb)

发言人刻意避免就这一议题发表看法。

3) Same English Words, either Affirmative or Negative in Chinese

(1) I'm new to the work.

这工作我是生手。(这工作我不熟悉。)

(2) The subway station is no distance at all.

地铁站近在咫尺。(地铁站一点儿也不远。)

(3) The computer was left intact, the money gone.

电脑还在,钱却不翼而飞了。

(电脑完好无损,钱却不翼而飞。)

(4) She is just as rich as most of the girls who come out to Britain.

跟那些出国到英国去的女孩比一比,她不见得穷到哪儿去。(她跟那些出国到英国去的女孩一样富有。)

(5) He had not the least difficulty in discovering the true cause of his present behavior.

他很容易就弄清了造成他目前这般境况的真正原因。(对他来说,弄清造成自己目前这般境况的真正原因一点不难。)

(6) When the world was a simpler place, the rich were fat, the poor were thin, and right-thinking people worried about how to feed the hungry.

世界原本没有这么复杂,那时候富人胖,穷人瘦,头脑正常的人在发愁:怎样才能让挨饿的人吃上饭。(世界原本很简单,那时候富人胖,穷人瘦……)

4) Double Negative for Emphasis in English

Double negative in English, as in Chinese, is used for emphasis. In this case we may either drop the negative words or keep the original depending on the idiomatic expression of the Chinese version.

(1) There is no rule that has no exception.

任何规则都有例外。

(2) There is not any advantage without disadvantage.

有一利必有一弊。

(3) It is impossible but that a man will make some mistakes.

人不会不犯错误(人人都会犯错误)。

(4) But then the two of you came into my world with all your curiosity and mischief and those smiles that never fail to fill my heart and light up my day.

后来,你们两个进入了我的世界,带来的种种好奇、淘气和微笑,总能填满我的心,照亮我的日子。

5) Roundabout Way of Expressing the Affirmative in English

This is an indirect way of expressing the strong emotion on the part of the speaker, and when translated into Chinese, the original mood should be properly kept.

(1) I couldn't feel better. 我觉得身体棒极了。

(2) He didn't half like the film. 他非常喜欢那部影片。

(3) If that isn't what I want to do! 我所要做的就是这个呀!

(4) I couldn't agree with you more. 我太赞成你的看法了。

(5) They didn't praise him slightly. 他们对他大加赞赏。

(6) He can't see his new roommate quickly enough. 他很想尽快见到新室友。

6) Some Traps in English Negative Structures

not...because: 并不是因为，不……因为……

（1）The engine didn't stop because the fuel was finished.

引擎并不是因为燃料耗尽而停止运转。

（2）She didn't attend the meeting because she wanted to.

她参加会议并不是因为她自己想去的。

（3）She doesn't teach because she knows the answer to all questions.

她之所以教书并不是因为她知道所有问题的答案。

（4）Don't go for looks because they can deceive. Don't go for wealth, even that fades away.

不要倾心于容貌，因为它们具有欺骗性，也不要倾心于财富，它也会消散。

cannot...too/over/much: 无论怎样……都不过分，应尽量，越……越好

（1）You cannot be too careful in driving.

开车时，越小心越好。

（2）The importance of this conference cannot be overestimated.

这次会议的重要性无论怎么强调也不过分。

all/every...not: 并非都

（1）All cities did not look like as they do today.

在过去，所有城市并不都像今天这样千篇一律。

（2）All graduates will not be appointed to do some office works.

大学毕业生并非都被分配去做办公室工作。

both...not: 两者不都

（1）But you see, we both cannot go at the same time.

但是我告诉你，我们俩不能同时都走。

（2）Both read the same Bible, and pray to the same God; and each invokes His aid against the other. The prayers of both could not be answered.

双方念的是同一本圣经，拜的是同一个上帝，但各方都要求上帝帮助去打倒对方。所以，双方的祈求不可能都得到满足。

It + be + adj. + noun + that + negative sentence: 再……也会

（1）It is a good workman that never blunders. 智者千虑，必有一失。

（2）It is a long lane that has no end. 路长必有弯，事久必有变。

（3）It is a wise man that never makes mistakes. 再聪明的人也会犯错误。

4.2.2 Negation in Chinese-English Translation

1) Negative in Chinese, Affirmative in English

（1）油漆未干！Wet paint!

（2）我完全没有成见。I have a completely open mind.

（3）我没有注意到他的暗示。His hint escaped me.

（4）白天一定要做的事，一定要说的话，现在都可不理。

All that one is obliged to do, or to say, in the daytime, can be very well cast aside now.

2) Affirmative in Chinese, Negative in English

（1）那简直就是个奇迹。

That is nothing less than a miracle.

（2）但当时我脑子里却是一片空白。

But at the time I thought of nothing.

（3）他们工作时总是互相帮助。

They never work without helping each other.

（4）这些细菌要在温度达到100℃时才会死亡。

These bacteria will not die until the temperature reaches 100℃.

3) Special Negative Chinese Expressions

（1）我认为他根本无法替自己的行为辩护。

I do not see at all how he can justify him for such a conduct.

（2）我相信他们是不会反对你的建议的。

I don't believe that they will oppose your proposal.

（3）她一直认为自己不比任何人干的活少。

She never thought she could be outworked.

4) Translation of Double Negative

(1) 我们必须不骄不躁, 向人民学习。

We must be free from arrogance and rashness and learn from people.

(2) 她要是不说话, 我还一直不知道她是外国人。

Until she spoke I had not realized she was a foreigner.

(3) 正如没经历过大事的人一样, 他是经不起成功也经不起失败的。

Like those of little experience, he was easily elated by success and deflated by failure.

Translation Practice 2:

I. Translate the following sentences, using the technique of negation:

1. History has never been kind to Iraq.

2. Slips are scarcely avoidable when you're new to your work.

3. You couldn't turn on TV without seeing a woman demonstrating a product.

4. National universities, the pride of the prewar educational systems, were closed to women.

5. It is a valuable work. I do not think anyone writes so well that he cannot learn much from it.

6. The students hesitate when confronted with the vast untouched area of English vocabulary and usage which falls outside the scope of basic textbooks.

7. 我真看不懂这篇矿业论文。

8 我到汽车站去接同学, 可是没有接到。

9. 科学家不承认权威是真理的最后根据。

10. 那城市及周围的地方是不冻港和无核区。

11. 她觉得她再也不能忍受同学的讽刺挖苦了。

12. 关于该地区的石油储量情况, 人们毫无所知。

II. Improve the following translations according to the original:

1. 在任何情况下, 能量既不能创造, 也不能毁灭。

In any case, energy can't be created or destroyed.

2. 我适应不了这儿变化无常的天气。

I can't adapt to the changing weather here.

3. 只有认识到 2005—2007 年这最初的三年是一个"实验"期，才能评估欧盟排放交易体系取得的成绩。

Only we understand that the first three years from 2005 through 2007 were a "trial" period can we evaluate the performance of the European Union's Emissions Trading System.

4. The modern technique has made it possible to keep liquid hydrogen from being dangerously explosive.

现代技术已能阻止液态氢发生危险的爆炸。

5. Liquids, except for liquid metal such as mercury, are not considered to be good conductors of heat.

除了液体金属如水银外，其他液体不被认为是热的良导体。

6. A university, which is often erroneously called the highest seat of learning, sounds as if it were the summit of knowledge.

大学听起来好像就是知识的巅峰，常常被人们错误地称为最高学府。

Unit 5 Translation Skill (3) Rendering of Passive Voice

The wide use of the passive voice is one of the outstanding features of the English scientific documents. However, the passive voice is less commonly used in Chinese due to its flexible syntax. Therefore, conversion of voice is often necessary in English-Chinese and Chinese-English translation.

5.1 Passive Voice in English–Chinese Translation

1) Converting into Active Voice

Keeping the original subject

(1) Efficiency is usually expressed as a percentage.

效率通常用百分数来表示。

(2) In radiation, thermal energy is transformed into radiant energy, similar in nature to light.

在辐射时，热能转换成性质与光相似的辐射能。

(3) Before 2008, China was not expected to become the No. 1 energy-consumer until 2015, but it is now the major energy consumer.

根据2008年之前的预计，中国到2015年不会成为第一大能源消费国，但现在已成为主要的能源消费国。

Subject → object, prepositional object → subject

(1) Large quantities of fuel are used by modern industry.

现代工业耗用大量的燃料。

(2) About 10% of the world' oil supply is met by unconventional oils, and that

number will increase.

非常规油约占世界石油供给的10%,这一比例将持续攀升。

(3) Global refinery construction continues to be driven by growth in the global demand for refined products.

全球对成品油不断增长的需求促使世界各地不断建设炼油厂。

Adverbial → subject, subject → object

(1) Mean monthly rainfall in this city is shown in Table 3.1.

表3.1列出了该城市平均降水量。

(2) A film of oil is inserted between the sliding surfaces of a bearing.

轴承的滑动面之间上了薄薄的一层油。

(3) Accordingly, the successor phrase-II exploration campaign was taken up during 2011—2012.

因此,2011—2012年开始后续第二阶段的勘探活动。

Adding a general pronoun as the subject

(1) Rubber is found a good material for the insulation of cable.

人们发现橡胶是一种用于绝缘光缆的理想材料。

(2) If one or more electrons are removed, the atom is said to be positively charged.

如果原子失去一个或多个电子,我们就说该原子带正电荷。

(3) It has been calculated that the concentration of H+ in water is 0.0000001 gram per liter.

有人计算过,水中H+离子浓度为每升0.0000001克。

2) Changing into a Predicative Structure

(1) Electronics is based upon an understanding of physical world.

电子学是以人们对物质世界的认识为基础的。

(2) Many casting defects are caused by expansion properties of sand.

许多铸铁缺陷是由沙子的膨胀性质而引起的。

(3) The high voltage section of the power supply is solid encapsulated.

电源的高压部分是固体密封的。

3) Converting into No-Subject Sentences

(1) It has been proved that induced voltage causes a current to flow in opposition to the force producing it.

已经证明,感应电压使电流的方向与产生电流的磁场力方向相反。

(2) Russia and the Caspian Sea region are expected to export more gas to the East and West.

预计俄罗斯和里海地区将向东部和西部地区出口更多的天然气。

(3) An oxidation number may be assigned to each atom in a substance by the application of simple rules.

应用一些简单的规则,可以给一种物质里的各原子指定氧化值。

4) Keeping Passive Voice in Chinese with 被 / 遭……、受……、为……所、加以……

(1) With the emergence of an electronic currency, every one of us would be affected.

随着电子货币的出现,我们每一个人都会受到影响。

(2) Sustainable management is seen as a practical and economical way of protecting species from extinction.

可持续管理被人们视为一种保护生物物种使之免于灭绝的实用又经济的办法。

(3) For a better understanding of the present invention, two embodiments will now be described by way of example, with reference to the accompanying drawings.

为了更好地理解本发明,两个实施方案现通过举例和附图加以说明。

5) Replacing by Other Structures

In many cases, however, passive voice in English cannot be rendered into good Chinese by means of the patterns mentioned above. Therefore, it is up to the translator to adjust or remold the whole structure, so as to bring out a proper and readable Chinese version. For example:

(1) He had been wedded to translation.

他与翻译工作结下不解之缘。

(2) Most trees are denuded of leaves in winter.

大多数树木冬天要落叶。

(3) The news was passed on by word of mouth.

众口相传,消息不胫而走。

(4) Not too much can or should be read into the percentages.

这些百分比不能说明太多的问题,也不应利用它们来说明太多的问题。

5.2 Passive Voice in Chinese-English Translation

Passive structures are less often used in Chinese than in English, so Chinese-English translation is mainly from the "active" to the passive voice. Generally, the Chinese passive structures can be classified into two patterns: sentences with or without the passive labels.

1) Chinese Sentences with Passive Labels

In translating such sentences, we may copy the English passive structure.

(1)他深受大家的尊敬,被选为执委会主席。

He is respected by all and was elected Chairman of the executive committee.

(2)我们的对外政策受到全世界人民的支持。

Our foreign policy is supported by the people all over the world.

(3)特别是2011年实现了非常规油气资源勘探重大突破,延长石油集团被列为我国首批40个矿产资源综合利用示范基地之一。

Especially in 2011, an important breakthrough was made in the exploration of unconventional oil and gas, therefore Yanchang Petroleum was listed as one of China's first 40 demonstration bases of comprehensively utilizing mineral resources.

However, not all Chinese sentences with passive labels should be translated into English sentences in the passive voice, especially when it comes to English intransitive verbs.

(1)老太太被风吹病了。

The old lady fell ill because of the draught.

(2)天太冷,水管都给冻住了。

It was so cold that the water pipes froze.

2) Chinese Sentences without Passive Labels

Sometimes sentences of this category seem to be active in structure, but actually passive in meaning.

(1)应当注意机器的工作温度。

Attention must be paid to the working temperature of the machine.

(2)这种杀虫剂效果良好,屡试不爽。

This new insecticide has proved effective every time it is used.

(3)地铁15号线于去年年底建成。

The construction of subway line 15 was completed at the end of last year.

(4)同时,建成了聚丙烯等重点项目,实现从"单一燃料型"向"燃料化工型"的成功转型。

Meanwhile, polypropylene and other major projects are completed, realizing the successful transformation from the mode of "single fuel" into "chemical fuel".

5.3 Some Chinese Expressions in Common Use

Some Chinese expressions may be conveniently translated into English by using the pattern "It be + p.p. + that clause."

(1)应该说,局势基本上是稳定的。

It should be said that the situation is basically stable.

(2)必须指出,有些问题还需要澄清。

It must be pointed out that some questions have yet to be clarified.

(3)众所周知,火药是中国古代的四大发明之一。

It is well known that gunpowder is one of the four inventions of the ancient Chinese people.

(4)有人预测,电脑和网络技术新的互动将会对未来工业产生巨大的影响。

It is estimated that the new interaction between computers and net technology will have significant influence on the industry of the future.

Similar structures we have:

It is asserted that... 有人主张……

It is believed that... 有人认为……

It is claimed that... 有人主张／断言……

It can't be denied that... 大家认为……

It is generally accepted that... 大家公认／一般认为……

It is generally considered that... 大家（一般人／人们）普遍认为……

It will be said... 有人会说……

It is noticed that... 人们注意到……

It is stressed that... 有人强调说……

It was told that... 有人曾经说……

It is understood that... 人们理解……

It is considered... 据估计（人们认为）……

It is declared that... 人们宣称（据宣称）……

It is said that... 据说……

It is hoped that... 希望……

It is learned that... 据闻……

It is reported that... 据报道……

It is supposed that... 据推测……

It must be admitted that... 必须承认……

It will be seen from this that... 由此可见……

It may be said without fear of exaggeration that... 可以毫不夸张地说……

Translation Practice:

I. Translate the following sentences, paying attention to the conversion of the voice:

1. At least two quarts of water are required daily by a normal individual.

2. Mineral oil is useful only when it is cleaned and separated into different commercial products.

3. Those who support the "nature" side of the conflict believe that our

personalities and behavior are largely determined by biological factors.

4. And it is imagined by many that the operations of the common mind can be by no means compared with the processes of scientists, and that they have to be acquired by a sort of special training.

5. New sources of energy must be found, and this will take time, but it is not likely to result in any situation that will restore that sense of cheap and plentiful energy we have had in the times past.

6. On the whole such a conclusion can be drawn with a certain degree of confidence, but only if the child can be assumed to have had the same attitude towards the test as the other with whom he is being compared, and only if he was not punished by lack of relevant information which he possessed.

7. 势能可以很容易地变为动能。

8. 电机发热问题的解决办法终于找到了。

9. 用煤和石油可以制成各种各样有用的东西。

10. 应该鼓励各地方政府尽快出台保护环境和提高能源效率的办法。

11. 一切科技成就都是建立在理性思维的基础之上, 没有理性思维就不能有科学。

12. 石油供应可能随时被切断; 不管怎样, 以目前这种石油消费速度, 只需 30 年左右, 所有的油井都会枯竭。

Ⅱ. Improve the following translations according to the original:

1. 人们目前只能利用一小部分太阳能。

At present, people can only use a small portion of solar energy.

2. 律师的结论是从证人提供的事实和证据中推断出来的。

The conclusion of the lawyer deduces from the facts and evidence provides by the witness.

3. 这个建筑设计融入主题乐园的元素, 给城市中心的公民提供一个购物、休闲和交往的空间。

This architectural design integrates the element of theme park, and provides the citizens in the city center with a space for shopping, entertainment and communication.

4. Policies on coal, especially on CO_2 and SO_2 emissions, are formulated and implemented.

煤炭、尤其是二氧化碳和二氧化硫的各种政策被制定并实施。

5. Even when the pressure stays the same, great changes in air density are caused by changes in temperature.

即使压力不变,空气密度的巨大变化是由气温的变化引起的。

6. It could be argued that the radio performs this service as well, but on television everything is much more living, much more real.

无线电广播同样也能实现这项服务,但还是电视屏幕上的节目更生动、真实。这一点可能会有争议。

Unit 6 Translation Skill (4) Rendering of Attributive & Adverbial Clauses

6.1 Attributive Clauses in English–Chinese Translation

English attributive clauses are usually complicated and long. There are two kinds of attributive clauses: restrictive and non-restrictive ones. An English sentence may be followed by an unlimited number of attributive clauses that stand on the right side of the word being modified, while a Chinese sentence allows only a limited amount of words preceding the word being modified. For example:

(1) This is the cat.

这是那只猫。

(2) This is the cat that killed the rat.

这就是那只捕杀了老鼠的猫。

(3) This is the cat that killed the rat that ate the cheese.

这就是那只捕杀了偷吃了奶酪的老鼠的猫。

(4) This is the cat that killed the rat that ate the cheese that lay in the house.

这就是那只捕杀了偷吃了放在房间里的奶酪的老鼠的猫。

(5) This is the cat that killed the rat that ate the cheese that lay in the house that Jack built.

这就是那只捕杀了偷吃了放在杰克修建的房间里的奶酪的老鼠的猫。

Apparently, Chinese versions (3) (4) (5) seem very awkward because all the information can't be put into a single sentence. Therefore, readable version should be somewhat like the following:

(3) 这就是那只捕杀了老鼠的猫。老鼠偷吃了奶酪。

(4) 这就是那只捕杀了老鼠的猫。老鼠偷吃了堆放在屋里的奶酪。

(5) 这就是那只捕杀了老鼠的猫。老鼠偷吃了堆放在屋里的奶酪。屋子是杰克盖的。

The following methods can be adopted in translating English attributive clauses:

6.1.1 Restrictive Attributive Clauses

1) Combination

It means placing attributive clause before the word being modified (the antecedent), with the aid of the Chinese "……的……" pattern.

(1) During construction, problems often arise which require design changes.

在施工过程中，常会出现需要改变设计的问题。

(2) Engineering is the profession that puts scientific knowledge to practical use.

工程学是一门将科学知识运用于实践的专业。

(3) Humans have the ability to modify the environment in which they live, thus subjecting all other life forms to their own peculiar ideas and fancies.

人类有能力改变自己的生存环境，从而使所有其他形态的生命服从人类自己独特的想法和想象。

2) Division

It means dividing the sentence into two, placing the attributive clause after the principal clause and repeating the antecedent being modified.

(1) Galileo was a famous Italian scientist by whom the Copernican theory was further proved correct.

伽利略是著名的意大利科学家，他进一步证明了哥白尼学说是正确的。

(2) Very wonderful changes in matter take place before our eyes every day to which we pay little attention.

非常奇异的物质变化每天都在眼前发生，这是我们几乎没有注意的。

(3) There will be television chat shows hosted by robots, and cars with pollution monitors that will disable them when they offend.

届时，将出现由机器人主持的电视谈话节目以及装有污染监控器的汽车，一旦这些

Unit 6　Translation Skill (4) Rendering of Attributive & Adverbial Clauses

汽车排污超标时，监控器就会使其停驶。

3) Amalgamation

It means combining the meaning of the principal clause and that of the attributive clause in a single Chinese sentence, usually for "there be..." pattern. Besides, there are some English complex sentences in which emphasis is laid on the attributive clause. In this case, the principal clause may be condensed into the subject/predicate of a simple sentence, taking the attributive clause as its predicate/object. For example:

(1) There are some metals which possess the power to conduct electricity and the ability to be magnetized.

有些金属既能导电，又能被磁化。

(2) There are events taking place at this time which dim our hopes and lessen the prospects.

目前发生的一些事情使我们觉得希望渺茫，前途黯淡。

(3) Good clock have pendulums which are automatically compensated for temperature changes.

好的钟摆可以自动补偿温度变化造成的误差。

(4) There is no guarantee that we will win the bid for power asset.

不能保证我们会赢得电力资产竞标。

6.1.2 Non-restrictive Attributive Clauses

1) Division

Translated into compound sentences by repeating the antecedents:

(1) The molecules exert forces upon each other, which depend upon the distance between them.

分子相互间都存在着力的作用，该力的大小取决于它们之间的距离。

(2) The most important form of energy is electrical energy, which is widely used in our daily life.

最重要的能源形式是电能，它广泛地用于我们的日常生活。

(3) The team member gave us a detailed introduction about the process of the research, which is very important to us.

项目组人员向我们详细介绍了研究过程,这对我们来说非常重要。

Translated into compound sentences by omitting the antecedents:

(1) The lungs are subjected to several diseases which are treatable by surgery.

肺易受几种疾病的侵袭,但均可经手术治疗。

(2) When I try to understand what it is that prevent so many Americans from being as happy as one might expect, it seems to me that there are two causes, of which one goes much deeper than the other.

为什么如此多的美国人不能如想象中那样幸福呢?我认为有两个原因,而且有深浅之分。

Translated into independent sentences:

(1) Nevertheless the problem was solved successively, which showed that the computations were accurate.

不过,问题还是逐一得到了解决。这说明计算是准确的。

(2) Engineers have had a direct role in the creation of most of modern technology—the tools, machines, techniques, and power source that make our lives easier.

工程师在绝大部分现代科技创新中发挥着直接的作用。例如,为使生活更加便捷,我们靠他们才有了各种工具、机器、技术和能源等。

2) Combination

(1) The tree, the branches of which are almost bare, is willow.

那棵树枝几乎光秃的树是柳树。

(2) Transistors, which are small in size, can make previously large and bulky radios light and small.

体积小的晶体管使得先前那种大而笨的收音机变得又轻又小。

6.1.3 Attributive Clauses Functioning as Adverbials

Sometimes, attributive clauses are not limiting the meaning of the noun they modify, but somewhat like an adverbial, so attributive clauses are not always translated into attributive clauses in Chinese. They should be translated according to the habitual use of the Chinese language.

Translated into Chinese adverbial clauses of cause:

(1) To make an atomic bomb we have to use uranium 235, in which all the atoms are available for fission.

制造原子弹，我们必须用铀235，因为这种铀的所有原子都会裂变。

(2) There is a steady shift of scientists from the pure to the applied field, where there are more jobs available, frequently more highly-paid and with better technical facilities.

科学家不断从理论科学研究领域转移到应用科学研究领域，因为后者能够提供更多的工作机会，而且通常待遇优厚，技术设施好。

Translated into Chinese adverbial clauses of result:

(1) There was something original, independent, and heroic about the proposal that pleased all judges.

这个提案富于创造性，独出心裁，很有魄力，所以评委都很喜欢。

(2) Solar energy is a clean and renewable power resource on the earth, which is widely used for generating electricity.

太阳能是地球上的一种清洁、可再生的能源，因此被广泛用于发电。

Translated into Chinese adverbial clauses of concession:

(1) The recent actions of DPRK, which have aroused universal disapproval of the world, are not given up by them.

虽然朝鲜近日的行动已激起全世界的普遍反对，但他们并没有放弃。

(2) Electronic computers, which have many advantages, cannot carry out creative work and replace man.

尽管电子计算机有许多优点，但是它们不能进行创造性工作，也不能代替人。

Translated into Chinese adverbial clauses of condition:

(1) There is a minimum size for the reactor at which the chain reaction will just work.

想要链式反应能够有效地工作，反应堆就必须有一个最合适的尺寸。

(2) Anyone who thinks that rational knowledge need not be derived from perceptual knowledge is an idealist.

如果认为理性知识可以不从感性知识得来,这个人就是个唯心主义者。

Translated into Chinese adverbial clauses of purpose:

(1) Workers have to oil the moving parts of the machine, the friction of which may be greatly reduced.

工人们必须给机器的转动部件加油,以便可以大大减少这些部件间的摩擦。

(2) Currently, every country in the world has trade barriers, which are designed to protect its economy against international market forces.

如今世界各国都设置了贸易壁垒,以保护本国经济免受国际市场力量的冲击。

Translated into Chinese adverbial clauses of time:

(1) The object whose weight is more than that of the water displaced will sink.

当物体的重量大于它排开的水的重量时,它就会下沉。

(2) Electrical energy that is supplied to a lamp can be turned into light energy.

当把电供给电灯时,它就会变成光能。

6.2 Attributive Elements in Chinese-English Translation

In Chinese, there is no attributive sentence but it is quite common to see the long attributive with "的" pattern. When translated, such long structure can be transformed into English attributive phrase, or clause, or an independent sentence. For example:

(1) 在我们肉眼看来似乎静止不动的一杯水中,却有数不清的水分子正在进行着大量的无规则的热运动。

Although the water in a glass (which) looks to be totally motionless to our naked eyes, a great deal of thermal movement of its countless molecules is going on disorderly inside.

(2) 当前我们迫切需要有一个装备优良、人员齐备、按照安全保护原则、本着一丝不苟的精神建立起来的先进核能实验室。

A well-equipped and well-manned nuclear-energy lab is badly needed at present. Such a lab, of course, must be advanced in technology and built in accordance with the principle of security as well as in the spirit of meticulous discretion.

Translation Practice 1:

I. Translate the following sentences, paying attention to the attributive clauses in English and the "……的……" pattern in Chinese:

1. You compare her with your English-women who wolf down from three to five meat meals a day and naturally you find her a sylph.

2. Now the integrated circuit has reduced by many times the size of the computer of which it forms a part, thus creating a new generation of portable minicomputers.

3. Unlike global warming and ozone depletion—which, if the political will was there, could be reduced by cutting gas emission—preserving bio-diversity remains an intractable problem.

4. Behaviorists suggest that the child who is raised in an environment where there are many stimuli which develop his or her capacity for appropriate responses will experience greater intellectual development.

5. The increasing speed of scientific development will be obvious if one considers that TV, space craft, and nuclear-powered ships, which are taken for granted now, would have seemed fantastic to people whose lives ended as recently as 1920.

6. 全世界的科学家都在寻找净化空气、防止空气受到各种有害工业废气污染的有效方法。

7. 一个不怕困难、百折不挠、坚持到底的科学工作者一定会在科研工作中取得辉煌的成就。

8. 过去,我们的企业一般不重视经济效益,广泛存在着劳动无定员、生产无定额、质量无检查、成本无核算的现象,造成人力、物力、财力的很大浪费。

II. Improve the following translations according to the original:

1. 那是2008年建于北京的一个设备优良的体育馆。

It was a gymnasium which was well-equipped and built in Beijing in 2008.

2. 这是一个基于人们对人的权利有共同认识，而世界上并不存在这种共同认识的假设之上的问题。

This is a question which assumes that there is an agreed account of human rights which the world does not have.

3. 文化被定义为包括人作为社会成员所获得的信仰、艺术、道德、法律、风俗以及其他能力和习惯的复合体。

Culture is defined as a complex whole which includes man's belief, art, morals, law, custom, and any other capabilities and habits as a member of society.

4. A body whose position changes with time is said to be moving.

据说，一个位置随时间而变化的物体在运动。

5. Nowadays it is understood that a diet which contains nothing harmful may result in serious disease if certain important elements are missing.

如今人们知道，如果缺少某些重要成分，不含任何有害物质的食物也会引起严重的疾病。

6. Certain types of hazardous household wastes have the potential which causes physical injury to sanitation workers, and contaminate wastewater treatment systems if poured down drains or toilets.

某些有害的家庭垃圾如果倒进下水道或马桶，有伤害环卫工人的身体，污染污水处理系统的可能。

6.3 Adverbial Clause in English-Chinese Translation

English adverbial clauses include adverbials of time, place, cause, condition, concession, purpose, result, and so on, and their sentence structures are flexible. The basic translation principle from English into Chinese is to arrange them in an order of subordinate clauses first and principle ones last, and omit some unnecessary conjunctive words, while adding connectives when necessary and rearranging the order according to the logic in translating Chinese adverbial clauses into English. Besides, sometimes those adverbial clauses can be interchanged in translating, such as from adverbial clause of time into that of place.

1) Adverbial Clauses of Time

Expressing the time relations by lexical means:

(1) Ice keeps the same temperature while melting.

冰在融化时,其温度保持不变。

(2) After he had completed the experiment, he got the results published in a key journal.

实验完成后,他把实验结果发表在了一个核心期刊上。

(3) Engineers face the challenge task of keeping up with the latest advances while working to shape the technology of the future.

在致力于未来技术发展的同时,工程师还面临着跟上最新技术发展的挑战。

Translated into Chinese adverbial clauses of condition:

(1) Turn off the switch when anything goes wrong with the machine.

如果机器发生故障,就把电门关上。

(2) A body at rest will not move till a force is exerted on it.

若无外力的作用,静止的物体不会移动。

2) Adverbial Clauses of Place

English adverbial clauses of place can also be translated into Chinese adverbial clause of condition.

(1) The materials are excellent for use where the value of the work pieces is not high.

如果零件价值不高,最好使用这些材料。

(2) Generally, air will be heavily polluted where there are factories.

一般来讲,哪里有工厂,哪里的空气就会严重污染。

3) Adverbial Clauses of Cause

Translated into corresponding Chinese clauses with "因""由于", and so on.

(1) As the moon's gravity is only about 1/6 the gravity of the earth, a 200-pound

man weighs only 33 pounds on the moon.

由于月球的引力只有地球引力的六分之一，所以一个体重200磅的人在月球上仅有33磅重。

(2) Because science and technology are progressing and changing so rapidly, today's engineers must study throughout their careers to make sure that their knowledge and expertise do not become obsolete.

因为科学技术在飞速发展和变化，工程师必须毕生不断学习以确保其知识和专业技能不过时。

Translated into Chinese principal clauses:

In this case, the principal clauses are turned into clauses of result by having "所以" etc. before them.

(1) Pure iron is not used in industry because it is too soft.

纯铁太软，所以不用在工业上。

(2) Since information is continuously sent into the system as it is become available, teletext is always kept up-to-date.

新获得的资料不断地输入，所以电传文字系统总是保持最新水平。

4) Adverbial Clauses of Condition

Translated into Chinese adverbial clause of condition, or clause of supposition:

(1) Should there be urgent situation, press the red button to switch off the electricity.

万一有紧急情况，请按红色按钮以切断电源。

(2) A body can more uniformly and in a straight line if there is no cause to change that motion.

如果没有改变物体运动的原因，那么物体将作匀速直线运动。

Translated into Chinese supplementary clauses:

(1) Any body above the earth will fall unless it is supported by an upward force equal to its weight.

地球上的任何物体都会落下来，除非它受到一个大小与其重量相等的力的支持。

(2) Sustainable management means humans should be able to use any species

of animal or plant for their benefit, provided enough individuals of that species are left alive to ensure its continued existence.

人类为了自身利益可以使用任何动物或植物物种,前提是每一物种有足够的个体存活下来,从而确保该物种得以延续。

5) Adverbial Clauses of Concession

Translated into corresponding Chinese adverbial clause of concession:

(1) Though the task was difficult, they managed to accomplish it in time.

虽然任务艰巨,他们还是设法及时完成了。

(2) I don't think you'll be able to understand this formula even when you finish college education.

即使你大学毕业了,我认为你也不会明白这个公式的意思。

Translated into Chinese "unconditional" clauses such as "不管""不论", etc.

(1) He got the same result whichever way he did the experiment.

不论用什么方法做实验,他所得到的结果都相同。

(2) All living things, whether they are animals or plants, are made up of cells.

一切生物,不管是动物还是植物,都是由细胞组成的。

6) Adverbial Clauses of Purpose

Adverbial clauses of purpose, when translated into Chinese, may either be placed before or after the principal clause of the sentence.

(1) Steel parts are usually covered with grease for fear that they should rust.

钢制零件通常涂上润滑脂,以防生锈。(为了防锈,钢制零件通常需涂上润滑脂。)

(2) A rocket must attain a speed of about five miles per second so that it may put a satellite in orbit.

火箭必须获得每秒大约五英里的速度,以便把卫星送入轨道。(为了能把卫星送入轨道,火箭必须获得每秒大约五英里的速度。)

6.4 Adverbial Clauses in Chinese-English Translation

Considering the different features in hypotactic English and paratactic Chinese, it is up to the translators to detect the implied meaning of the Chinese sentence and bring it out in the English version. The following are some typical examples.

（1）她不老实，我不能信任她。

Since she is not honest, I cannot trust her.

（2）向上的力与向下的力相等，气球就保持在这一高度。

The force upward equals the force downward so that the balloon stays at the level.

（3）开发油气资源是生产活动、经济活动，政府不宜随意干预。

Developing oil and gas resources is a productive and economic activity, so it shouldn't be interfered arbitrarily by the government.

（4）没有完善的技术服务市场，走"众人拾柴火焰高"发展道路只是句空话。

The development path that "many hands make light work" would mean nothing if there were no perfect technical service markets.

（5）与此同时，能源资源环境约束强化，经济发展受到更多制约条件，中国必须把能源安全作为战略的重中之重。

Meanwhile, due to the further restrictions on energy resources and environment as well as more constraints on economic development, China must take energy security as a strategic priority.

Translation Practice 2:

I. Translate the following sentences, paying attention to the adverbial clauses:

1. Electricity is such a part of our everyday lives and so much taken for granted nowadays that we rarely think twice when we switch on the light or turn on the radio.

2. These facts will remain true whether we are dealing with the application of psychology to advertising and political propaganda, or of medical science to the problem of overpopulation or old age.

3. Sometimes, tests do not compensate for gross social inequality, and thus do not tell how able an underprivileged youngster might have been had he grown up under more favorable circumstances.

4. 电是一种非常重要的能量，没有它，现代化工业就不能发展。

Unit 6 Translation Skill (4) Rendering of Attributive & Adverbial Clauses

5. 一条新的定理必须经过实践的检验以后，才能肯定它是否有价值。

6. 我们把自主创新作为未来发展的主要驱动力，走出一条资源节约、环境友好、社会和谐的可持续发展道路。

II. Improve the following translations according to the original:

1. 回顾龙源电力的风电发展历程，从技术层面归纳，主要有三个解决方案。

Review of the development course of wind power of China Longyuan Power and summarize from the technical level, there are three solutions.

2. 在研究中，如果数据集过小或者样本类型不足会导致深度学习算法的过拟合。

In the study, the deep learning algorithm will be over-fitted if the data set is too small or the sample type is insufficient.

3. 中国本周二公布了新能源汽车购车补贴计划的细则，旨在促进国内汽车工业发展，并减少车辆排放量。

China Tuesday released details of its green-car subsidy program in order to boost the nation's auto industry and cut vehicle emissions.

4. The achievements we have made so far are only a new beginning, so the future arduous tasks still require us a long way to go.

我们目前取得的成就只是一个新的开端，因此，未来艰巨的任务还要求有很长的路要走。

5. Due to the unreasonable energy structure, and a long period of coal-fired heating in winter in the region, air pollution is becoming more and more serious in recent years.

由于该地区不合理的能源结构，和冬季较长的燃煤采暖期，近年来大气污染严重。

6. With the deep integration of advanced information technologies such as mobile Internet, big data and cloud computing with the energy industry, the intelligent level in the energy development and utilization has improved rapidly.

随着先进信息技术，如移动互联网、大数据、云计算等，与能源产业的深度融合，能源开发利用的智能化水平快速提升。

Unit 7 Translation Skill (5) Rendering of Long Sentences

Translation of a typical long English/Chinese sentence usually consists of two stages and seven steps:

<u>Stage I: Comprehension</u>

Step 1: Draft a skeleton of the long sentence,

Step 2: Infer the main idea from the context,

Step 3: Distinguish between the principal and subordinate elements,

Step 4: Find out the interrelations between principal and subordinate clauses.

<u>Stage II: Presentation</u>

Step 5: Enter on a tentative translation of each sentence division,

Step 6: Rearrange and balance,

Step 7: Finish touches.

Let's analyze the above seven steps in the following illustration.

It is nothing else than impurities parentally inherent in ore that seriously affect the quality of the latter, which is formed as a result of geological vicissitudes including diastrophic movement, eruption of volcano, sedimentation, glaciations and weathering etc., under the action of which phylogenic rocks, volcanic complex, aqueous rocks, sedimentary rocks etc., come into being, some of which exist in a stage of symbiosis, the main cause of the absence of pure rocks in nature, wherein lies the reason for the need of separation technology and apparatus, namely, ore-dressing devices and equipment, so far impotent to meet the requirements of metallurgical industry the scientists make every endeavor to elevate to a new high by laser separation.

Unit 7 Translation Skill (5) Rendering of Long Sentences

矿石是由地质变化形成的,这些地质变化包括地壳变迁运动、火山爆发、沉积作用、冰川作用和风化作用等。在上述地质变化的作用下,形成了火成岩、火山杂岩、水成岩和沉积岩等。正是岩石中的天然固有杂质影响了矿石的质量。上述这些岩石中,有些处于共生状态——这也是自然界没有天然纯矿石的主要原因。人们之所以需要矿石分离技术与器械,即选矿装置与设备,其原因盖出于此。迄今为止,分离技术和器械尚远不能满足冶金工业的需要,科学家们正全力以赴,利用激光分离机把冶金工业提高到一个新水平。

7.1 Long Sentence in English-Chinese Translation

1) Following the original order

(1) The proportion of the various ingredients which go into concrete, the way it is mixed, and even the water which is used are very important to the finished material.

制作混凝土所用的各种配料的比例,搅拌的方法,乃至所用的水,对成品材料来说都是十分重要的。

(2) Engineers should be curious about the "how" and "why" of natural and mechanical things and creative in finding new ways of doing things, and able to analyze problems systematically and logically and to communicate well.

工程师应该对自然和机械事物的方式和原因充满好奇心,能够创造性地发现开展工作的新方法,能够有步骤、有逻辑地分析问题,并善于沟通交流。

(3) You have all heard it repeated that men of science work by means of induction and deduction that by the help of these operations, they, in a sort of sense, manage to extract from nature certain natural laws, and that out of these by some special skill of their own, they build up their theories.

你们都多次听说过,科学家是用归纳法和演绎法工作的,他们用这种方法,在某种意义上说,力求从自然界找出某些自然规律,然后,他们根据这些规律,用自己的某种非同一般的本领,建立起他们的理论。

2) Reversing

(1) Does it really help society, or the victim, or the victim's family, to put in jail a

man, who drove a car while drunk, has injured or killed another person?

一个人酒醉后开车,压死或压伤了另一个人,就将这个人关进监狱,这样做对社会、受害者或受害者的家庭是否真的有好处呢?

(2) The high-quality wind power equipment couldn't be produced without the solid theoretical foundation, qualified materials and equipment, necessary test and practices.

如果没有扎实的理论研究基础、合格的材料和设备以及必要的试验和实践基础,很难生产出合格的风机设备。

(3) Global operating rates of refineries may trend downward if there are not delays in projects scheduled to come on stream in the 2014—2015 timeframe, which, based on the history of refinery project development, is quite likely.

从炼油厂项目的发展历史来看,如果2014—2015年预计投入生产的项目不推迟,全球炼油厂的运营率很可能会有所下降。

3) Breaking up

(1) Plastics is made from water which is a natural resource, coal which can be mined through automatic and mechanical process at less cost and lime which can be obtained from the calcinations of limestone widely present in nature.

塑料是由水、煤和石灰制成的。水是天然资源;煤是用自动化和机械化的方法开采的,成本较低;石灰是由燃烧自然界中广泛存在的石灰石得来的。

(2) Aristotle could have avoided the mistake of thinking that women have fewer teeth than men, by the simple device of asking Mrs. Aristotle to keep her mouth open while he counted.

亚里士多德误认为妇女牙齿数目比男人少。这种错误,他本来是可以避免的,而且办法很简单。他只要请亚里士多德夫人把口张开,他亲自数一数就行了。

(3) Human beings have distinguished themselves from other animals, and in doing so ensured their survival, by the ability to observe and understand their environment and then either to adapt to that environment or to control and adapt it to their own needs.

人类把自己和其他动物区别开来。与此同时,人类还具有观察和了解周围环境的能力。他们要么适应环境,要么控制环境,或根据自身的需要改造环境。人类就这样一代代地生存下来。

4) Inserting Marks like Dash or Bracket

(1) Of all languages, English has the largest vocabulary, perhaps as many as two million words, and one of the noblest bodies of literature.

在所有语言中,英语的词汇量最大——大约200万个单词——也是具有最丰富的文学宝库的语言之一。

(2) If you go to visit Nobel's old residence, the house in which the great chemist remained a bachelor throughout his life, you will catch sight of a shelf laden with experimental records.

如果你参观诺贝尔的故居——在那座房子里,这位伟大的化学家过了一辈子的独身生活——你将会看到一个堆满实验记录的书架。

(3) The need to produce goods and services at quality levels previously thought impossible to obtain in mass production and the spreading use of participatory management techniques will require a work force with much higher levels of education and skills.

提供高质量的产品和服务的需要(而过去则认为大批量生产是不可能做到这一点的),以及参与型管理技术的推广使用,都对劳动力提出更高的教育和技术要求。

5) Recasting According to Logic and Chinese Habit

(1) Dr. Smith resumed the activities of anti-cancer experiment begun in 1945 and financed by the Federal government as soon as he snapped from his original disappointment at repeated failures, which had resulted in its forced suspension.

1945年,史密斯医生开始着手由联邦政府资助的抗癌实验。他由于屡遭失败而感到沮丧,被迫终止了实验工作。现在他又重新振作起来,恢复了抗癌实验活动。

(2) It has been more than one year since Alfred Jackson, a 38-year-old Brooklyn plumber, was shot and killed by a neighbor because Mr. Jackson wanted to park in the spot where the man was walking his dog.

阿尔弗莱德·杰克逊,38岁,生前是布鲁克林一名水暖工人。有一天他想在邻居遛狗的地方停放汽车，竟被邻居开枪打死。这件事发生已有一年多了。

(3) But without Adolf Hitler, who was possessed of a demoniac personality, a granite will, uncanny instincts, a cold ruthlessness, a remarkable intellect, a soaring imagination and—until toward the end, when drunk with power and success, he overreached himself—an amazing capacity to size up people and situations, there almost certainly would never have been a Third Reich.

然而，如果没有阿道夫·希特勒，那就几乎可以肯定不会有第三帝国。因为阿道夫·希特勒有着恶魔般的性格、花岗石般的意志、不可思议的本能、无情的冷酷、杰出的智力、深远的想象力以及对人和时局惊人的判断力。这种判断力使他最后由于被权力和胜利冲昏了头脑而自不量力，终于弄巧成拙。

7.2 Long Sentence in Chinese-English Translation

Long sentences are also a headache for the translator in Chinese-English translation. Since there is a great disparity between Chinese and English sentence structures, we should learn to tackle them discriminatingly. The usual methods adopted in translating long Chinese sentences into English include the change of clause order and division/breaking up. For example:

(1)"十五"期间要突出重点，搞好开局，着重加强基础设施和生态环境建设，力争五到十年内取得突破性进展，同时使科技、教育有较大发展。

During "the Tenth Five-Year Plan" period, we need to place emphasis/stress on key projects for a good beginning of the program. Construction of infrastructure and protection of the ecological environment should take priority, and we should strive for major breakthroughs within five to ten years. At the same time, we hope to develop science, technology, and education considerably.

(2)中国是世界上最大的发展中国家，中国政治、社会稳定，经济持续发展，市场将更加开放，市场环境不断改善，这将给包括欧盟企业在内的国际工商界带来更多的投资、贸易机会。

As the largest developing country in the world, China is proved to have stable political and social environment, constant economic growth and ever-opening market as well as ever-better market atmosphere, which is also going to generate more investment and trade opportunities for international business circles including EU businesses.

（3）一些大型电力集团公司将业务延伸到了设备制造，并要求本集团公司投资的风电场主要采用本企业生产的风机设备，这不仅造成了不公开的竞争环境，而且不利于风电产业的持续健康发展。

Some large power groups expand their businesses to equipment manufacturing, and require the group-invested wind farms to use their own equipment, which not only causes the closed competitive environment, but also damages the sustained and sound development of the wind power industry.

（4）我们不但要有一个农林牧副渔布局合理、全面发展、能够满足人民生活和工业发展需要的发达的农业，还要有一个门类齐全、结构合理、能够满足社会消费和整个国民经济发展需要的先进的工业。

Version 1: We not only need a developed agricultural system with a rational distribution and all-round development of farming, forestry, animal husbandry, side-line production and fishery, meeting the needs of the people's life and expanding industry, but also an advanced industrial system which has complete range and rational structure and meets the needs of consumers and the expansion of the whole national economy.

Version 2: We not only need a developed agricultural system but also an advanced industrial system. The former requires a rational distribution and all-round development of farming, forestry, animal husbandry, side-line production and fishery to meet the needs of the people's life and expanding industry, while the latter should have a complete range and rational structure to meet the needs of consumers and the expansion of the whole national economy.

Translation Practice:

I. Translate the following long sentences, paying attention to their structure:

1. It is not that the scales in the one case, and the balance in the other, differ

in the principles of their construction or manner of working but that the latter is a much finer apparatus and of course much more accurate in its measurement than the former.

2. There is just the same kind of difference between the mental operation of a man of science and those of an ordinary person as there is between the operations and the methods of a baker or a butcher weighing out his goods in common scales, and the operations of a chemist in performing a difficult and complex analysis by means of his balance and finely graduated weights.

3. As a resort, conditions permitting, we may seek at home medical service, namely, diagnosis and treatment from abroad, to use professional terminology, telesatdiag, as compared with vis-à-vis consultation, say, in an ill-equipped, poorly staffed hospital, particularly on an acute, severe or, in physician's view, unidentified case, undoubtedly a most effective therapeutic device available.

4. The secret of the moon remained unveiled until the latter half of the twentieth century due to the lack of lunar space carrier, for a series of questions concerning fuel, material, safe landing, propelling mechanism and particularly electronic computation etc. were too intricate to solve under the technical conditions early in this century, which have since been undergoing profound change and greatly improving.

5. 历史业已证明，人类对于资源的认识、开发和利用，以及利用资源制造生产工具的能力，是社会生产力发展水平的重要标志，也在一定程度上决定了一定的社会基本结构和发展形态。

6. 中华人民共和国成立60多年来，矿产资源勘查开发取得了巨大成就，探明了一大批矿产资源，建成了比较完善的矿产品供应体系，为中国经济的持续快速协调健康发展提供了重要保障。

II. Improve the following translations according to the original:

1. 过去10年，全球非水可再生能源消费量年均增长15.9%，明显高于能源消费总量1.9%的增速。

In the past decade, the annual growth rate was 15.9% of the global non-water renewable energy consumption, which obviously exceeded the 1.9% in total energy consumption.

2. 大多数风电开发企业重发展速度和建设规模,轻发电量水平、运行管理和营利能力。

Most wind power development enterprises pay more attention to the speed of development and the scale of construction while disregarding power generation level, operation management ability and profitability.

3. 健全法律法规、强化技术支撑、加强政策引导,切实抓好节地节能节水节材,提高资源综合利用效率。

We must improve relevant laws and regulations, give a bigger role to technologies, strengthen policy guidance, do well in the conservation of land, water, energy and raw materials, and enhance the efficiency of integrated resources consumption.

4. Until such time as mankind has the sense to lower its population to the point where the planet can provide a comfortable support for all, people will have to accept more "unnatural food".

除非人类有意识把人口减少到这样的程度:地球能为所有人提供舒适生活,否则人们将不得不接受更多的"人造食品"。

5. There are several reasons why Kissinger no longer appears to be the magician the world press had made him out to be, an illusion which he failed to discourage because, as he would admit himself, he has a tendency toward megalomania.

有几个原因说明基辛格不再是魔术师般的人物,这是国际新闻界曾经对他的渲染,而他也没有阻止人们制造这种错误印象,因为他自己也承认有一种自大狂的倾向。

6. Although protection of the environment has long been a matter of basic state policy for the government, it is an undeniable fact that efforts to improve the environment have largely failed to match destructive forces working against them.

尽管保护环境一直是该政府制定的一项基本国策,然而不可否认的是,改善环境的种种努力很大程度上不能与逆势而上的破坏活动相匹配。

Unit 8 Translation of Scientific Papers

8.1 Introduction to English for Science & Technology

1) Linguistic Features

Stylistically

English for science and technology (EST) writing is a kind of formal writing, avoiding all colloquial expressions. For example, "establish, gradually, terminate, verify" are used instead of "build/set up, step by step, end/finish, prove/bear out".

Syntactically

It has rigorous grammatical structure, and in most cases is rather unitary. Frequently used are indicative sentences, imperative sentences, complex sentences, long sentences, the relative pronoun "that" or "which", and "It be + adj. (past participle) + that ..." sentence patterns and passive voice.

According to John Swales from the University of Leeds, about 1/3 of sentences are passive voice in EST. For example, in EST, it is more proper to say "Attention must be paid to the working temperature of the machine" but not "You/We must pay attention to... machine."

Morphologically

It is featured by high specialization, the use of technical terms and jargons, unambiguous implication, the fixed sense of the word, more compound words, Latin and Greek words, contracted words, noun clusters (nominalization), etc.

Rhetorically

Unlike literary English (LE), EST writings seldom employ such literary rhetorical devices as hyperbole, figures of speech, personification, antithesis, irony, humour, etc. Look at the following two discourses which all describe man but by different devices of expression.

EST

Man is metazoan triploblastica chordate vertebrate pentadactyle mammalian eutherian primate, hominid homo. The main outlines of each of his principal systems of organs may be traced back like those of other mammals to the fishes.

人类归属于脊索动物门类、脊椎动物亚门类、哺乳纲、真兽亚纲、灵长目、人科、人属。他是后生的三胚层五趾动物，其每一个主要器官系统的轮廓都像其他哺乳动物一样，可以追溯到鱼类。

LE

What a piece of work is a man! How noble in reason! How infinite in faculty! In form and moving how expressive and admirable! In action how like the angle! In apprehension how like a god! The beauty of the world! The paragon of animals!

人类是一件多了不起的杰作！多么高贵的理性！多么伟大的力量！多么优美的仪表！多么文雅的举动！在行为上多么像一个天使！在智慧上多么像一个天神！宇宙的精华！万物的灵长！

Besides, non-verbal language is also very popular in EST such as signs, formulas, charts, tables, photos, etc. for the sake of accuracy, brevity, and clarity.

2) Translation of Technical Terms

（1）Transplant

dataphone 数据送话机　　　microwave 微波　　　splashdown 溅落

flowsheet 流程图　　　holography 全息摄影（术）

（2）Pictographic Translation/Morphotranslation

English letters are often used to name the objects which are similar to the letter in shape. This kind of terminology is generally morphotranslated:

Choose the characters in translation that can denote the shape of the original object and ／ or English letter:

    T-square 丁字尺   I-column 工字柱

    T-track 锤形径迹   H-beam 工字梁

    U-bend 马蹄弯头   V-slot 三角形槽

    U-steel 槽钢   V-belt 三角皮带

    Y-curve 叉形曲线   X-brace 交叉支撑

    Z-iron 乙字铁   O-ring 环形圈

Keep the letter not translated, but add a character "形" to it, which is more popular in translation:

    A—bedplate A 形底座   D—valve D 形阀

    C—network C 形网络   M—wing M 形机翼

Keep the letter not translated, use the letter to stand for a concept:

    N-region   N 区（电子剩余区，即电子导电区）

    AT-cut   AT 切片（切割方向与光轴成 35° 角的晶片）

    L-electron   L 层电子（原子核外第二层的电子）

    X-ray   X 射线（波长为 10—610—10 厘米的电磁波）

(3) Transliteration

It is to deal with proper nouns (especially the names of people and places, trademarks, etc.) and coinage where no existing Chinese expression is available.

    quinine 奎宁   clone 克隆   Pentium 奔腾（计算机微处理器）

    volt 伏特   Citroen 雪铁龙   nylon 尼龙

(4) Transliteration and free translation

    kilowatt 千瓦   decibel 分贝

8.2 Translation of Paper Title

Title is often featured in nominalization with concise, precise, formal language. Compare the following two versions:

（1）科技翻译方法初探

A: Preliminary Study of Methods of Scientific Translation

B: Methods of Scientific Translation

（2）机器翻译系统可靠性探讨

A: Discussion on Reliability of Machine Translation System

B: Reliability of Machine Translation System

（3）自然资源与环境的研究

A: Research on Natural Resources and Environment

B: Natural Resources and Environment

（4）论建筑学与现代科学技术

A: On Architecture and Modern Scientific Techniques

B: Architecture and Modern Scientific Techniques

（5）论公关工作在全面质量管理中的作用

A: Function of Public Relation Work in Total Quality Control

B: Function of Public Relation in Total Quality Control

（6）关于建筑产品质量问题的法律思考

A: A Consideration from the Angle of Law on the Problems in Quality of Building Products

B: A Consideration from the Angle of Law on the Quality of Building Products

（7）论劳动力市场需求约束条件下的经济模式

A: The Economic Model Restrained by the Condition in Market Demands of Labour Force

B: The Economic Model Restrained by Market Demands of Labour Force

8.3 Translation of Abstract

An abstract is a statement summarizing the important points of a text at the beginning of a document, such as a scientific paper. It is a concise and accurate representation of the contents of a document, in a style similar to that of the original document. It is a short description, or a condensation of a piece of writing.

1) Linguistic Features of Abstract

(1) Diction:

Abstract is precise, concise, and more formal in wording. Care must be exercised to avoid ambiguity, and redundant phrases such as: "the authors studied" "in this work" "the paper concludes by", etc. should be avoided if possible.

(2) Grammar

* Use the third persona: "the author" "the paper" is preferred to "I", or "we".

* Use simple past tense to indicate things done in the past or to describe the things the author has done.

* Use simple present (perfect) tense for the conclusion drawn from the work.

* Use future tense (be to do) for the aim/goal/purpose of the paper.

* Use more passive voice than active voice.

(3) Sentence Structure:

* Use more indicative sentence, verb close to the subject.

* Use brief and informative sentences.

* Sentences with an average length at about 12 words are likely to yield a readable abstract.

* Avoid the sentence beginning with a phrase or clause; more often start with the important fact/active voice.

(4) Arrangement:

All abstracts, barring possibly those of exceptional length, should consist of one paragraph only. This should be a coherent paragraph, and not a series of disjointed sentences.

2) Formation and Sentence Pattern of an Abstract:

Topic sentence:

(1)本文介绍／讨论／详细论述／提出……

This paper/article describes (introduces/discusses/elaborates/focuses on/raises/proposes)…

…is/are studied (discussed/shown/presented/introduced/proposed/analyzed/explained) in this paper/article

(2) 作者提出/试图……

The author /writer presents/ endeavors the problem...

(3) 本文的目的是解释/介绍/讨论……

The purpose/objective of this article /contribution is to explain/describe/ discuss/introduce...

(4) 本文的主要目的有三……

This paper has three main objectives:...

(5) 该项科研项目致力于……

This research project is devoted to...

(6) 本文提供了有关……的详细信息

Detailed information is presented about...

(7) 本文对……作了研究。

A study has been made of...

(8) 本文（论文、报告等）论述（详细说明、调查、包含、涉及）了以下问题：

This paper (thesis, report, etc.) addresses (specifies, examines, covers, is concerned with etc.) the following questions: ...

(9) 本文（文章、报告、论文、文献、著作、报道等）阐述（报告、说明、总括、讨论、概述、展开、调查、分析、评价）了……的结果（方法、作用）。

This paper (article, report, thesis, document, work, account etc.) describes (reports, explains, outlines, summarizes, discusses, surveys, develops, investigates, analyzes, etc.) the results (approaches, roles, etc.) of ...

Supporting sentences:

(1) 实验/实例 显示/表明/证实……

Experiments/examples demonstrate/confirm/show...

(2) ……被提出/验证/引自/分析……

...are /is given/verified/derived from/analyzed...

Concluding sentences:

(1) 结果（发现、数据、实例等）表明（显示出，提出等）……

Results (examples/findings) show (demonstrate/indicate/suggest) ... / It shows.../The results ... are given/presented...

(2)结论为……/我们的结论是……

This concludes that.../ It is concluded that.../ We conclude that...

(3)作者建议……

The author proposes.../...is proposed (by the author).

(4)现已发现（观察、证实）……

It has been found (observed, shown proved, etc.) that...

(5)这个方法有望对……很有用。

The approach (method, etc.) promises to be very useful for...

(6)希望本研究对未来的……有一定的指导意义。

It is hoped that the present study would be of some guidance to the future...

3) Problems in the Translation of Abstract

Using improper and wordy expressions

(1)本文提出了一种新的计算机辅助翻译方法。

A: A new computer-aided translation method is put forward in this paper.

B: A new computer-aided translation method is presented (in this paper).

(2)本文对提高打印速度和印字质量提供了一种机辅设计手段。

A: This paper presents a CAD method for increasing the printing speed and the printing quality.

B: This paper presents a CAD method for increasing the printing speed and improving the printing quality.

Using colloquial or informal style

(3)本文主要研究平面结构的可动性。

A: This paper mainly studies the movability of plane components.

B: This paper principally studies the movability of plane components.

(4)作者所讲的内容对通讯工程师来说是很感兴趣的。

A: The content that the author talks about is of great interest to communications engineers.

B: What this paper describes is of great interest to communications engineers.

Inflexible translation by following the original order and expression

As we know, nominalization structures are often used in the form of phrases to express an action, so as to make it more concise, definite, compact and objective. For example:

（5）本文对该设备的性能进行了分析。

A: The performance of this device is analyzed (in the paper).

B: An analysis of the performance of this device is made.

（6）简要介绍了磁悬浮列车的基础知识。

A: Fundamentals of a maglev are briefly introduced.

B: A brief introduction is given to the fundamentals of a maglev.

（7）本文对最近推荐的一种方案作了研究。

A: This paper studies a recently-recommended scheme.

B: A study has been made of a recently-recommended scheme.

Starting the sentence with a phrase or clause but not the important fact

（8）从实验数据可以确定反应堆余烬的燃料消耗量。

A: From data obtained experimentally, fuel consumption in a reactor core was determined.

B: Fuel consumption in a reactor core was determined from data obtained experimentally.

Verb is far away from the subject

（9）本文针对当前我国对外经济法规汉英翻译的一些实际问题，探讨了以翻译规律来规范对外经济法规汉英翻译的可能性。

A: This paper, aiming at some obvious errors in translating current China's foreign economic laws and rules, discusses the possibility of governing the C-E translation of those documents.

B: This paper discusses the possibility of governing the C-E translation of current China's foreign economic laws and rules after analyzing some obvious errors in translating.

Monotonous structure

（10）环流反应器在工业上正得到越来越广泛的应用，对其进行深入研究对于此类反应器的设计与放大具有重要意义。对环流反应器的流动、混合及传质特性参数随表观气速、液相物性、系统压力和反应器尺寸等操作条件的变化关系进行了综述。介绍了各特性参数的测量方法,并指出了这些方法的优缺点及可能存在的误差。对环流反应器的流动、混合及传质特性的数学模型进行了评述,并在此基础上对环流反应器研究的发展前景进行了展望。[何广湘等,2008(1):66]

[Original version]

Airlift loop reactors (ALRs) have been widely used in industry, so the investigation of ALRs is very important for their design and scale-up. The effects of operating conditions, such as superficial gas velocity, liquid properties, system pressure, reactor size, on the behavior of ALRs were discussed and the measuring methods for the reactor behavior were introduced, also their deficiency was pointed out. The mathematical models of flow behavior, mixing and mass transfer in ALRs were reviewed.

[Suggested version]

It is very important to study the design and scale-up of airlift loop reactors (ALRs) due to their wide application in industry. Therefore, this paper discusses the effects of operating conditions, such as superficial gas velocity, liquid properties, system pressure, reactor size, on the behavior of ALRs. It also introduces the measuring methods for the reactor behavior and their deficiency as well. Eventually, the mathematical models of flow behavior, mixing and mass transfer in ALRs were reviewed.

4) Translation Principles

* Be aware of the purpose of the abstract to be translated.

* Be familiar with the entire document whose abstract is to be translated.

* Be succinct in wording.

5) Ways of Translating Chinese Abstracts

Breaking-up

(1)本文对去污工艺的化学、物理过程进行了理论分析,认为氧化去污机理是6种化学反应的联合进行,还提出了去污剂选择的理论依据。

This paper has analyzed theoretically the chemical and physical process of decontamination. The author holds that mechanism of decontamination consists in combination of six chemical reactors. The scientific bases for selecting decontaminants are proposed as well.

（2）机器翻译技术及各类翻译软件已在很大程度上改变了传统的人工翻译模式，降低了翻译的劳动强度，提高了翻译效率，如将其用作外文翻译的辅助工具，用途的确非常广泛，尤其科技翻译受益匪浅。但因受制于关键技术及涉及跨文化交流的内涵，机译及翻译软件无法区分文本的感情色彩，因而它们注定不能取代人工翻译的主宰作用。

Machine translation technology and various translation softwares have dramatically changed the traditional human translation mode. They have reduced labor intensity in human translation and enhanced translation efficiency. Indeed, they can serve various purposes if used as auxiliary tools on translation of foreign languages, especially that of science and technology. However, machine translation and translation software are unable to differentiate sensational elements due to constraints on technology crux and implications of cross-cultural exchange. Hence, they cannot replace the dominant role of human translation.

Combination

（1）本文比较了STM和ATM。结果表明ATM是BISDN的基础。

A comparison between STM and ATM shows that ATM will be the basis of BISDN.

（2）本文提出了解决这一问题的新方法。这种方法简单而又切实可行。

A new method for solving this problem is presented, which is simple and practicable.

（3）煤矿水灾害会对煤矿企业造成巨大的损失。选择有效的煤矿水灾害救治系统可以最大程度降低其损失。

Coal-mine flooding will bring great economic losses and casualties to coal enterprises, so an effective rescuing system can greatly reduce such losses.

6) Sample Analysis

In terms of sentence structures, there are often two types of Chinese abstracts.

One is featured in one or two long sentences with some fixed structure/patterns like "基于/针对……,阐述/分析……,剖析/论证……,提出/提供……". In this case, the translator should clearly analyze the logical relations among different elements, and divide them into different coherent sentences. The other is written with several short sentences but sometimes with subjects/conjunctions omitted, so the combination method is often adopted.

[Sample 1]

从信息论的角度分析了一个典型的两步量子直接通信方案的安全性,计算了该量子直接通信过程中攻击者 Eve 所能获得的信息量及在 Eve 进行攻击后合法通信者所能接收的信息量,为合法者对量子直接通信的安全性判定和对敌手的检测提供了一定的依据和标准。[周南润等,2008(4):389]

[Original version]

The security of a typical scheme of the two-step quantum direct determinant communication is analyzed from the aspect of information theory. The amount of information which the eavesdropper and the legal receiver can get is calculated, which can serve as a criteria for checking Eve and estimating the security of quantum direct communication between legal communicators.

[Analysis]

This is a quite typical Chinese abstract consisting of only one sentence with the fixed pattern but without obvious subject: 分析了……计算了……提供了…….

The above translation turns one Chinese sentence into two English passive sentences. And subjects are either chosen from the original or added to conform to English norms. The second sentence is a much longer containing one passive voice and one active voice, and two "which", so the structure is a little complex for an abstract. It is better to divide it into two parts. What is more, the two sentences are mainly literally translated by following Chinese paratactic structure without clearly indicating the logical relations with some connectives. Besides, "criteria" is a plural form; here it should be a single form (criterion).

[Suggested version]

This paper first analyzes from the aspect of information theory the security of a typical scheme of the two-step quantum direct determinant communication. Then the amount of information that the eavesdropper and the legal receiver can get is calculated. Therefore, the research can serve as a criterion for checking Eve and estimating the security of quantum direct communication between legal communicators.

[Sample 2]

提出了一个利用一束单光子对话的方案。在方案中，利用两个不同的幺正操作对光子态进行编码，并且从一束光子中选择较大的子集进行窃听检查，该方案能够有效地抵御截取再发送袭击。此外，由于利用单光子没有利用EPR对，因此该方案是很实际的。该方案是绝对安全的。（计新等，量子光学学报2008/3）

[Original version]

We propose a quantum dialogue scheme using a batch of single photons. In the scheme, we encode the states of the single photons with the secret message by two different unitary operations, and select randomly a sufficiently large subset of photons from the batch to check eavesdropping, so our scheme can resist the intercept-and-resend attack efficiently. In addition, our scheme is practical because it uses single photons instead of EPR pairs. The conclusion shows that the scheme is unconditionally secure.

[Analysis]

This is another typical Chinese abstract with a few short sentences. It is written with a combination of Chinese and English structures, having subjects omitted in the first two sentences but many conjunctions used (并且……此外……由于……因此)

The above translation follows the original order and logical relation with some repeated addition of subjects (we... we... our... our... the conclusion…) and more conjunctions (so, instead of) according to the implied logic. The problems are as follows:

First of all, the whole abstract lacks variety with all the four sentences in active voice. And the second sentence is longer, wordy, illogical and ungrammatical. Besides, the connective "so" is used improperly in that context in both meaning and structure. Finally, EPR is better given a full name for facilitating readers' reading. And the style is informal.

[Suggested version]

This paper proposes a quantum dialogue scheme using a batch of single photons. The scheme is to encode the states of the single photons with two different unitary operations, and check eavesdropping to a sufficiently large subset of photons from the batch. It is proved that our scheme can resist the intercept-and-resend attack efficiently. In addition, it is practical and unconditionally secure by using single photons instead of electron paramagnetic resonance (EPR) pairs.

Translation Practice:

I. Put the following passage into Chinese/English.

1. Professional literatures have been regarded as "intangible assets" of the whole world because they are, on the one hand, the summary, generalization, and development of the achievements obtained on the basis of previous experiences or studies; and on the other hand, they have been accumulated and handed down from generation to generation. In this sense, therefore, all kinds of literature are records of precious research findings and academic achievements, and the crystallization of human civilization.

2. 科技文献是用文字、图形、符号、声频和视频等方式记录人类科学技术知识的载体,是人类文明的产物。科技文献具有四大功能,即信息承载功能、知识体现功能、创新支撑功能和教育培训功能。科技文献资源是一个发展着的动态体系。由于科技突飞猛进的发展,其综合与分化的趋势日益明显,使得科技文献呈现出数量激增,老化加速,类型复杂,形式与内容广泛、分散、交叉、渗透的状况。

II. Improve the following translations according to the original:

本文以我国能源结构优化、治理大气污染为背景,首先阐述了推进"煤改气"工程在治理大气污染方面的作用。其次探讨了"煤改气"在京津冀地区应用过程中出现的天然气供不应求、调峰压力增大、采暖成本增加等问题。最后提出了可行性建议。

Under the background of our country try to optimize energy structure, control air pollution, this paper first explains the effect of "coal to gas" project in the treatment of air pollution. Then it discusses the problems in the application, such as the demand for natural gas exceeds the supply, the pressure of peak shaving increases, the heating cost rises and so on. And finally it offers some practical suggestions.

Part II

Academic Writing and Presentation

Unit 1 General Introduction to Academic Writing

1.1 Definition of academic writing

Academic writing is a general term. It may be a term paper for a university course, a published article in an academic journal, or a thesis or a dissertation for a university degree. It is concerned with academic research in one way or another, and intended to inform the audience of the research topic, purpose, method, results, findings, conclusions, and recommendations. There are two basic criteria that make up academic research writing. First of all, academic writing has to have a precise and clear topic, which is related with some academic science. Secondly, it has to be structured according to the academic requirements.[1]

1.2 Reasons for academic writing

One obvious reason is that the experience familiarizes the students with the conventions of academic research ethics, the rudiments of scholarly writing, the conventions of footnote and bibliography. A second reason is that students become familiar with the library through the "learn by doing" method. Even the simplest library is an intricate storehouse of information, bristling with indexes, encyclopedias, abstracts. How to ferret out from this maze of sources a single piece of needed

---

[1] Taylor, N. Academic Writing: A Handbook for International Students[M]. London: Routledge, 2014.

information is a skill that students learn by doing actual research.

Third, writing the research paper is a complicated and trying exercise in logic, imagination, and common sense. As the authors chip away at the mass of data and information available on their chosen topics, they learn:

* how to think,

* how to organize,

* how to discriminate between worthless and useful opinions,

* how to summarize the gist of wordy material,

* how to budget their time,

* how to conceive of a research project from the start, manage it through its intermediary stages, and finally assemble the information uncovered into a useful, coherent paper.

There are other benefits too. Academic research writing teaches an appreciation for the intricacies and difficulties of academic research. Discovering for themselves the complexity of apparently simple and straightforward subjects, students learn to appreciate the labors of the researcher and the scholar.[1]

1.3 Characteristics of Academic Writing

Academic writing is in the standard written form of the language. It has one central point or theme with every part contributing to the major argument. Its objective is to inform rather than entertain. There are 7 characteristics of academic writing that are often discussed.

1) Complexity

Complexity in academic writing comes from the fact that the standard written form of the English language, which is compulsory to use, is different form the language we speak daily. The vocabulary used by the written language is more varied than the one used in conversations. It also uses more complicated words that are not

---

[1] Taylor, N. Academic Writing: A Handbook for International Students[M]. London: Routledge, 2014.

normally used when one talks with someone face to face.

Adding affixes to existing words (the base) to form new words is quite common in academic writing, that is to say, there is huge use of complex formation of words. The most common prefixes used to from new verbs in academic writing are: re-, dis-, over-, un-, mis-, out-. Prefixes usually do not change the class of the base word. But suffixes usually do change the class of the word. The most common suffixes are:-ise, -en, -ate, -(i) fy.

In addition, technical words and semi-technical words are widely used in academic writing. Technical words are specialized vocabulary used just in one discipline or some limited areas. They, with precise and narrow meanings, are often derived from Latin and Greek roots or compounded from existing words, whose meaning is well-known and unchanged. For instance, pharmaceutics（制药）, turbine （涡轮机）, thermodynamics（热力学）. Besides, some words are derived from ordinary English and have different specific meanings in their different technical fields. For instance, the word "carrier" in ordinary English means a person or business that carries goods or passengers from one place to another for payment. However, in medicine it refers to a person or thing that carries and passes diseases to others without him-/herself or itself suffering from it; in military it refers to a vehicle or ship which carries soldiers, weapons, planes, etc.; in physics it refers to a hone or an electron capable of carrying an electric charge; in mechanics it refers to a container for carrying; in chemistry it refers to a usually inactive accessory substance.[①]

What's more, the phrases in the written language are noun-based and those in speaking language are verb-based. The grammatical aspect of the written language is also different because we don't normally use in speaking so many subordinate clauses and passives. This also makes academic writing different from face to face communication or other types of writing.

2) Formality

In close connection with complexity is formality. Since an academic paper is

---

① 郭继荣. 学术论文写作与发表[M]. 西安:西安交通大学出版社,2012.

written for professionals in the same field and in many cases intended for publication in professional or academic periodicals, and the purpose is to present accurate information, the style of writing tends to be formal. Under no circumstances will academic writing make use of colloquial expression that you consider natural in daily dialogues you have with friend or colleagues. The degree of formality should thus be pretty high. The formality is achieved through its diction, sentence structure, and format.

The rhetorical context of the academic paper determines that its diction should be both precise and appropriate. Informal expressions (colloquialisms and slang expressions) are usually frowned upon as being unprofessional and out of place in academic writings.

Nominalization is a linguistic term which means the process of transforming a verb, an adjective or a clause into a noun or nominal group. Generally speaking, nominalization in academic English can be classified into lexical nominalization and clausal nominalization which can be further divided into nominal clauses, gerunds and infinitives. It is a function that not only helps you to create variety in your writing, but also prevents you from repeating the same verb/word over and over again.

The structure of nominalization is independent of the dynamic subject manifested in spoken form. By taking the actions and logical process of nominalization, academic English is organized by abstract concepts. Thus, more impartiality and objectiveness are achieved in this way.

It can also make the text more concise by packing a great deal of information into a few words. As a consequence of using nominalization, your writing will be more compact, objective and formal. The usage of nominalization marks the formality of academic writing.

It is true that sentence structures for the academic paper tend to be complex sentences because complex ideas demand complex sentences to express them clearly and accurately. It often adopts longer and more complex sentences to show relationships (temporal, spatial, contrastive, and causal) between ideas. Strings of short and simple sentences will give readers unfavorable impression of lack of intellectual maturity. On the other hand, wordy, tangled and excessively leaden sentences are unwelcome because they hinder understanding, obscure meaning, and do not serve the purpose of a research.

While the ideas being presented are the most important in an academic paper, the appearance and format it uses also participate in the making of meaning. So, an academic paper should have an aesthetically pleasing appearance: typewritten or printed on good-quality white paper, free from errors, and clear, with easy-to-read diagrams, figures, and tables. Different academic disciplines follow different styles or conventions in documentation. Academic papers in the humanities, especially in literature and language studies, generally use the MLA (Modern Language Association) style, while writing in the social sciences uses the APA (American Psychological Association) style. Research papers in the natural sciences and mathematics employ other documentation styles, of which the most widely used is the CBE (Council of Biology Editors) style. In colleges and universities, the MLA style and the APA style are most widely used.[①]

3) Objectivity

Academic writing is all about expressing opinions, yet these opinions need to be presented as objective, and educated position based on sound evidence. It therefore has fewer words that refer to the writer or the reader. This means that the main emphasis should be on the information that you want to give and the arguments you want to make.

How to Avoid Personal Language?

* Avoid using personal pronouns such as "I" "me" "myself" "we" "our" "us" "you" "your" to refer to yourself or the reader.

[①] Slade, C., Robert P. Handbook for Writing Research Papers, Reports, and Theses[M].北京:外语教学与研究出版社, 2011.

* Avoid using judgmental words that indicate your feelings about a subject, such as approving, excellent, positive, negative, and suspicious.

* Avoid using words that are emotive, such as complacent, convincing, disappointed, and joyful. Avoid providing no evidence for the presented arguments and use references to indicate sources.

4) Explicitness

Academic writing is explicit about the relationships in the text. Furthermore, it is the responsibility of the writer to make it clear to the reader how the various parts of the text are related. The effectiveness of a text is increased if the logical relationships exist between the various parts of the text. These relationships can be made explicit by the effective control of information flow and the use of different signaling words.

Signaling Words Commonly Used in Academic Writing

Time / order	At first, first, firstly, in the first place, to begin with, finally, eventually, in the end, lastly, in the second place, later, next, second, secondly
Cause and effect	Therefore, thus, hence, since, so, so that, in consequence, consequently, as a consequence, as a result, accordingly, because, because of, for this reason, owing to, due to
Comparison/similar ideas	In the same way, similarly, in comparison
Contrast/opposite ideas	Whereas, nevertheless, on the other hand, in spite of, despite, however, in contrast, on the contrary, but, yet
Explanation/ equivalence	Namely, that is to say, in other words, to be more precise, simply put
Addition	In addition, what is more, apart from this, as well as, besides, furthermore, moreover, not only...but also, too, as well, additionally
Generalization	In general, normally, generally, as a rule, for the most part, on the whole, in most cases
Emphasis	Chiefly, notably, especially, in particular, particularly, in detail, in depth

Continuation

Stating the obvious	Clearly, naturally, obviously, surely, it goes without saying, as one might expect, after all
Support	Actually, as a matter of fact, in fact, indeed
Summary /conclusion	Finally, in brief, in conclusion, in short, overall, to sum up, in summary, last but not least

5) Conciseness

In academic writing you need to be concise when you use information, dates or figures. Academic papers seldom use decorative locutions, which lead to redundancy. Keep in mind:

* Be specific and precise.
* Use the most straightforward term and reduce unnecessary words.
* Delete descriptive, redundant words or colloquialisms.
* Use the specific terminology of your subject.
* Become a ruthless editor, cutting out as much dead-wood as possible.

6) Hedges

Particularly, academic writing is simply to convey facts and information. However, it is now recognized that an important feature of academic writing is the concept of cautious language, often called "hedging" or "vague language". There are three reasons for the use of hedges.

Firstly, the authors tone down their statements in order to reduce the risk of opposition by hedging. Secondly, they want their readers to know that they do not claim to have the final word on the subject. Thirdly, hedges may be understood as politeness strategies in which the authors try to appear humble rather than arrogant or all-knowing. Hedging is a rational interpersonal strategy which supports the authors' position, builds author-reader relationships and guarantees a certain level of acceptability in a community.

Hedges

Modal lexical words	Seem, tend, appear, indicate, suggest, assume, estimate, propose, speculate, suppose
Modal auxiliary verbs	Will, would, may, might
Modal adverbs	Probably, perhaps, likely, unlikely, presumably, virtually, largely, practically, conceivably, somewhat, somehow, roughly, apparently, essentially, primarily, often, usually, frequently, sometimes
Modal nouns	Assumption, probability, claim, suggestion, likelihood, estimation
Introductory phrases	To our knowledge, on the evidence of, according to, on the basis of, based on, for the most part, to a great extent
Compound hedges	It might be suggested that, it may suggest that, it seems that, it would indicate that, this seems reasonable to assume, it probably indicates
"If" clauses	If anything, if necessary, if true, if possible, if any

7) Responsibility

In academic writing you must be responsible for and must be able to provide evidence and justification for, any claims you make. You are also responsible for demonstrating and understanding of any source texts you use, that is to say, you had better integrate the evidence you have gathered into your paper. This is done by paraphrasing and summarizing what you read and acknowledging the source of this information or ideas by a system of citation.

1.4 Classification of Academic Papers

An academic paper is a formal printed document in which authors present their views and research findings on any deliberately chosen topic. It is variously known as "report paper" "research paper" "thesis" or "dissertation". No matter what kind of paper may actually belong to, the task of the authors may, in most cases, be the same: to do research on any particular topic, and then gather information on it, and report their research findings.

Academic papers assigned in universities and colleges or any other research institutions are generally of the following four types: 1) report paper; 2) research paper; 3) term paper; and 4) thesis or dissertation.

1) Report Paper

The report paper summarizes and reports the findings of the authors on a particular subject. The authors may not give their own opinions on the issue, nor evaluate the finding, but merely catalog them in a sensible sequence. For instance, a paper listing the opinions of statesmen or politicians during the debate over a certain event would be a report paper. Likewise, a paper that chronologically narrates the last days of a personality would also be a report paper.

2) Research Paper

A research paper usually deals with a relatively specific topic with a comparatively narrow subject and intelligent, well-informed, interesting, and original in its conclusions. It draws its materials from many sources with the aim to assemble facts and ideas and study them to draw new conclusions as to facts or interpretations, or to present the materials in the light of a new interest.

Research papers are or can be the most important and reliable sources for textbooks, monographs, and all other documentary works. A complete research paper is usually composed of the following elements: title, author, affiliation, abstract, keywords, introduction, theoretical analysis and/or experimental description, results and discussion or conclusion, acknowledgments, references, etc.

3) Term Paper

Different from the report paper and research paper, a term paper mainly refers to the paper written after a specific course is learned or at the end of the term, so its contents usually should be in line with the course requirements and under the instruction of the course instructor. Since this type of paper is always written and handed in at the end of the term, it is also called "course paper".[1]

---

[1] 刘承宇, Patton, M.D. 学术英语写作教程[M]. 北京:中国人民大学出版社, 2015.

4) Dissertation or Thesis

Many students and young researchers are often confused with terms such as thesis, dissertation and paper because they can all be translated into *lun wen* (论文) in Chinese. In this book, the word "dissertation" is used to refer to "a long essay that you do as part of a degree or other qualification" (John Sinclair, 2002: 540) that you are studying for, that is to say, a BA or MA. The term "thesis", by contrast, is used to refer to "a long piece of writing, based on your own ideas and research that you do as part of a PH.D degree" (John Sinclair, 2002: 2034). ①

Thus, if the essay is a part of a BA or MA degree, we call it a dissertation; if it is a part of a PH.D degree we call it a thesis. As a result, you have different terms for different pieces of writing that you do during your university studies: a BA dissertation, A MA dissertation, a PH.D thesis, a term paper. The distinction between thesis and dissertation made here is in line with the British educational tradition. It must be pointed out that in the United States of America the use of these two terms is the other way around.

In general, a dissertation or thesis is a lengthy, formal paper, especially one written by a candidate for the master's or doctoral degree at a university or a research institution. Included in a dissertation (thesis) are more or less such sections as acknowledgments, abstracts (both in Chinese and English), introduction and/or literature review, methodology, data collection and data analysis, findings and conclusions, suggestions or future work, etc. As is often required, a dissertation for the degree of MA or MS should be of something new, while a thesis for the degree of PH.D should be of something original and creative. The dissertation, or thesis, should be independently completed, under the supervisor's guidance, by the candidate himself/herself, reflecting the candidate's own research findings.

---

① 黄国文,葛达西,张美芳. 英语学术论文写作[M]. 重庆: 重庆大学出版社, 2014.

1.5 Procedures of Academic Paper Writing

1) Negotiating a Topic

To negotiate a topic means you must first locate a good research subject, and then resort to one or a combination of the following exercises: following personal interests, talking with other people, and reading source materials.

Firstly, interest is the best teacher. Therefore, you should focus on what you are interested in and would like or make a further study when deciding on a research topic. If you are not interested in a topic, you may perform poorly. In this case, you should choose something that seems to promise you real value, something that you have always wanted to learn more about. The more you probe into the topic, the more you will find the topic interesting, the deeper understanding you will gain, and the better you will write.

Furthermore, as the Chinese saying goes, "One evening's conversation with a gentleman is worth more than ten years' study." A good research topic may come from a talk with your fellow students, instructors or friends. Something said might trigger an idea for a promising research topic. As you talk with each other, ideas are given and questions are asked, which result in elaboration and collaboration through interaction.

In addition, a good library usually contains excellent sources for finding a topic. You can turn to books, periodicals, Internet resources for ideas.

2) Narrowing down the Research Topic

Once ideas are formulated, they should be analyzed, replenished and finally sorted out after a long process of critical reading and thorough reconsideration. Usually, a suitable topic can be formulated and finally decided on by following five general rules. (1) It should be a topic within the reach of you and capable of being finished within the assigned or suggested time limit. (2) It should be topic of practical value for the specialty or the development of economy or science in general. (3) It should be a topic for which sufficient materials and documents can be made available either through readings or through investigations. (4) It should bear being tested theoretically and experimentally if your research is experimentation and investigation in nature as science demands thoroughness, accuracy and objectivity. (5) It should be a topic free from your personal bias or preference even if it may be a topic of humanistic nature. [①]

As we know, if the research topic is too broad, we may feel difficult to write a research paper concisely and completely. Therefore, narrowing down the research topic is essential when we decide on writing our research paper. Working through the following questions can help you narrow your topic:

* What broad subject are you considering?

* What five areas can you divide the subject into?

* Which of these five areas is more interesting to you?

* When you have made a choice, break it down once again. What are another five sub-subdivisions?

* Which of these aspects interest you most? Do you think this aspect will interest your readers?

* What in particular would you like to know about it? What specific questions might you ask about it?

3) Considering Audience and Purpose

By considering the audience and purpose we mean analyzing the "Call for Papers". Generally speaking, the instructors at colleges and universities who assign the papers are the primary and immediate readers. When a paper is aimed at publication, the possible readers of the journal to which your paper is to be submitted are targeted, or the possible participants of the conference you are going to attend are targeted.

As a writer, you should anticipate the needs or expectations of your audience in

---

① 胡庚申. 英语论文写作与国际发表[M]. 北京: 外语教学与研究出版社, 2014.

order to convey information or argue for a particular claim. Knowing your audience helps you to make decisions about what information you should include, how you should arrange that information, and what kind of supporting details will be necessary for the reader to understand what you are presenting. It also influences the tone and structure of the document.

4) Familiarizing Yourself with the Background

Once you have chosen a research topic and totally consider the anticipations of your audience, you are supposed to start to learn more about the subject area. There are a number of ways of widening your knowledge of the research topic and other background information. A traditional way is library research. Go to the university library and check the catalogues by subject search, keyword search, author search, or title search. Another way of searching for information related to your research is to use Internet selectively and wisely. You can use < http:// www. Google.com> or <http:// scholar. Google. Com/intl/zh-CN/> or <https://www.sciencedirect.com/> or http://www.cnki.net/ or <http:// www. Baidu. com > to start with.[1]

You can also follow existing approaches to the problem by reading papers dealing with similar problems. From those writings you can get a general idea of what has been done in the field so that you know where to start for your own research. You can even replicate existing studies.

5) Reading the Relevant Literature and Taking Notes

One of the problems with young researchers is that they do not read enough and as a result they have little or no idea of what can be done or should be done as a project for a dissertation. They should understand that some of the previous writings should be studied very carefully and in detail, and that they can just go through other writings to get some general information. In other words, they should learn to read

---

[1] Coyle, William & Law, Joe. Research Paper [M]. 16th ed. 北京: 北京语言大学出版社, 2015.

selectively.

While you are reading and digesting other people's ideas, you usually have three stages to go through. In the first stage, you try to understand as much as you can and try to follow the train of thought provided by the author. You then critically read and identify the strong points, e.g. new ideas, findings, and weak points or areas to be further explored. Finally, you should decide on how to use the existing writings. It may be an important paper that you have to mention in your review of the literature. It may give your ideas and theoretical supports for your arguments. You may base your research on the work that is reported in the existing writing or you may replicate this research.

Taking notes is an important step in preparing for your academic writing. During the process of your research and writing, you need to read many reference materials, review other people's researches, and summarize previous studies and existing research findings. When you are taking notes, identify the organizing pattern of the reading materials and try to organize your notes in a way that allows for later use. To save bother later, you could develop the habit of recording bibliographic information in a master list when you begin looking at each source (don't forget note book and journal information on photocopies) . Then you can quickly identify each note by the author's name and page number; when you refer to sources in the research paper you can fill in details of publication easily from your master list. Keep a format guide handy. You should try as far as possible to put notes on separate cards or sheets. This will let you label the topic of each note. Not only will that keep your notes have a clear focus, but it will also allow for grouping and synthesizing of ideas later. It is especially satisfactory to shuffle notes and see how the conjunctions create new ideas.

In addition, it is a good choice to leave lots of spaces in your notes for comments of your own questions and reactions as you read, second thoughts and cross-references when you look back at what you've written. These comments can become a virtual first draft of your paper. You will also find useful theoretical assumptions and ideas, arguments, definitions of concepts, which you need to refer to by quoting directly or indirectly or by paraphrasing or summarizing. Remember whether paraphrasing or summarizing, you should always give credit to the cited author.

6) Working out an Outline

An outline is a useful framework that assists in the organization and writing of the research paper. Preparing an outline can help you evaluate the materials and decide which piece of information is relevant to the purposes of the paper and discover the connections between the pieces. Drafting can only be started on the basis of a perfect outline. It is true that you may use whatever form you find comfortable working out an outline. There are three main types of outlines: the topic outline, the sentence outline and the paragraph outline. The most important principle for an outline's form is consistency. Never mix or combine the different formats in a paper. Use one type of outline exclusively.

The topic outline

In a topic outline, every heading is a noun phrase, or its equivalent (e.g. a gerund phrase), or an infinitive phrase. Keep all headings brief and clearly related to the major heading. The advantage of such an outline is that it is brief and quickly identifies the main points of discussion.

The sentence outline

A sentence outline uses complete sentences for all entries with correct punctuation used after each entry. This type of outline requires more planning and writing than the topic outline, but its completeness will prove more useful when one begins to write the paper. Complete sentences from the outline can be incorporated into the paper as topic sentences, which speeds up the writing.

The paragraph outline

In this type of outline, every section is a paragraph, which provides a summary of the main parts of the outline. This form is useful mainly for long papers whose individual sections can be summarized in whole paragraphs; it is seldom recommended by instructors for ordinary college paper. [①]

An outline can use either alpha-numeric (usually with Roman numerals) form or a decimal form. Alternating patterns of upper and lower case letters with alternating progressions of Roman and Arabic numerals mark the level of subordination within the alpha-numeric form of the outline. Progressive patterns of decimals mark the levels of subordination in decimal form of outlining. Based on the decimal accounting system, this outline form permits an unlimited number of subdivisions through the simple addition of another decimal place. The decimal form has become the standard form in scientific and technical writing.

(1) Producing a First Draft

A good draft is necessary to organize all the facts and ideas related together in a logical and systematic way, that is, in a manner that all the details and related facts appear in the paper as a whole. With the outline done, now it is time to get ready to produce a first draft. There are some useful tips for writing the first draft:

* Reread the notes and information as you have grouped them for outlining, to see what comes to your mind first. If you feel you can begin with the introduction, start from the beginning. If you have difficulty in writing the introduction but feel more inclined to write some other parts, begin with those, and you may return to the introduction later. At this stage, the most important thing is to make the writing happen and to put down your ideas as quickly as you can.

* During writing, do not stop to polish your sentence or find perfect word every now and then. You need to have a high tolerance for the imperfectness of what you have produced at this initial stage of the writing process. Particularly, you should not be too concerned with your grammar, spelling, punctuation and exact wording. The main concern is to get the ideas out according to the outline. Remember you are working on a draft that you will revise considerably later.

---

① Gastel, B. & Robert A. D. 科技论文写作与发表教程. [M]. 6th ed. 曾剑芬, 译. 北京: 电子工业出版社, 2018.

* Refer to your outline often as you draft. If you find yourself losing track or direction, stop writing and reread what you have written and compare it to the outline. If you are stuck somewhere in your writing, referring to your outline can help. Of course, you can revise your outline during the whole writing process, adding new ideas or changing the order of parts.

* When drafting, leave enough spaces or margins on the paper for later ideas or revision. Certainly, the computer and word-processing technology make it much easier for you to experiment with ideas.①

(2) Editing and Proofreading

When following the outline prepared to complete the writing of a research paper, you have to bear in mind that even if you are an exceptionally skillful author, you also have to make considerable revisions. If at all possible, you may put your draft away for one or two days to get some distance from it. What looks good when you are fully occupied in writing may not look the same way after a day or two. Before you revise, you need to read your draft thoughtfully and critically. In most cases, revision work would continue until the last minute for the submission of the paper. It is advisable to revise the paper from its general layout to the minute omissions and mishaps in language use. The following are some useful tips for editing and proofreading:

* Use the spell check function of your word processor (e.g. Microsoft Word, Word Perfect) to proofread your paper from beginning to end. You should look up any word the spell checker highlights but you are not absolutely sure of.

* Read carefully from the beginning to the end once again, and keep a close eye on the spelling and other mechanics. Although computer spell checkers may help find out misspellings, they cannot detect those words that are correctly spelt but wrongly used. For instance, when you put "always" wrongly in the place of "all ways" or "fare" for "fair", spell checkers cannot find them out. Also, proofread carefully for capitalization because spell checkers cannot catch a book title that has not been

---

① 程爱民, 祁寿华. 英语学术论文写作纲要[M]. 上海:上海外语教育出版社, 2005.

capitalized or underlined appropriately.

* Use either American spelling or British spelling consistently throughout your paper and do not mix.

* Check your punctuation carefully even though you have done it by using a spell checker. Try to make sure that all your punctuation marks and other mechanics are correct.

The experience of writing, as put by many experienced writers, is more like taking a steep trail in a wild mountain with frequent zigzagging twists and turns; just when it appears that you are retracing old ground, you are actually rising to a new level which commands a different and probably more beautiful view.[①]

Reflections and Practice

I. **Brainstorm ideas for one of the topics below. Then write down the outline for an academic paper on the topic.**

1. Air Pollution in Urban Areas

2. Effects of the One-Child Policy

3. The Importance of Punctuality

4. The Necessity of Recycling

5. Responsibilities of College Students

II. **Rewrite the following sentences in a formal style.**

1. I began to feel more confident of myself.

2. He is too young to handle this problem.

3. He has not much money and not many friends.

4. He spoke loudly so that everyone could hear him.

5. I showed in Chapter 1 it is not an easy question.

6. The time isn't enough for us to catch the next train.

7. He is the person that is well-known all over the country.

8. Every major city keeps changing and Lisbon is not an exception.

---

① 刘振聪, 修月祯. 英语学术论文写作[M]. 北京: 中国人民大学出版社, 2013.

9. Concerning your accommodation, there are several possibilities.

10. You can see clearly the difference between the treated and untreated specimens.

11. There have been a great number of complaints for the service in the canteen.

12. To come to the conclusion, I would like to say that everyone should be able to work if they want to.

13. Significantly, even at this late date, Lautrec was considered a little conservative by his peers.

14. When a patient is admitted to a psychiatric inpatient unit, the clinical team should avoid the temptation to start specific treatments immediately.

15. Effective vaccines prevent such hazards, but only if a social organization could make sure that all potential mothers are vaccinated in good time.

Unit 2 Title, Author, Affiliation and Key Words

2.1 Title

Title is indeed text in miniature. Unclear or boring research paper title creates a negative impression on the readers and brings absolutely no desire to read the work further. Thus, a creative and an attention-grabbing research paper title will encourage the reader. Title, which appears first in a research paper, is one of its major components. It should be formulated so that the reader would get the idea of what he/she will be reading about.

1) General Functions

An academic paper title has three functions in general. Firstly, it generalizes the text by summarizing the central idea of the paper concisely and correctly. Secondly, an interesting title may draw particular attention among professionals. Thirdly, it helps to facilitate the retrieval as it is the first piece of information that reader acquires and a good title can help the reader in his/her search for information to be indexed frequently.

<u>Generalizing the text</u>

A title should summarize the central idea of the paper concisely and correctly. It must be consistent with the contents of the document, and be highly representative of the central idea of the paper. By glancing at the title and incorporating the abstract, the reader will immediately know what is mainly dealt with in the paper.

Attracting the reader

An interesting title may draw particular attention among professionals, for only when readers are interested in the title will they decide to read the whole paper. Ideally, the title, by reading it, any professional reader can see whether the paper is worth reading at all.

Facilitating the retrieval

A good title can help the reader in his search for information. During the process of paper retrieval the title is always the first piece of information the reader acquires. A title serves as an important index of information retrieval to meet the needs of extensive paper communication and information dissemination.[①]

2) Topic vs. Title

Research paper title is one of the major components of your research paper. It should be formulated so that the reader would get the idea of what he/she will be reading about. Sometimes students mix up 2 different notions—academic paper topic and academic paper title. Let us analyze the difference between them.

Academic paper topic is a wider notion, either given by your professor or chosen by yourself. It presents the area that you will investigate. However, academic paper title is the formulation of your investigation area. The purpose of a title is to attract the readers. That is one of the reasons why an academic paper title should be laconically formulated.

A research novice usually chooses too broad a topic. A good way to avoid this problem is to choose a general topic first and then narrow it to a smaller and more feasible title. For example:

* Chemistry

Chemical Processes

Improving Chemical Processes

Oxygen in Improving Chemical Processes

---

① 李桂荣. 英语学术期刊论文写作原理与实务（经管卷）[M]. 天津: 南开大学出版社, 2008.

Roles of Oxygen in Improving Chemical Processes

* **Computer**

Computer Virus

Computer Virus Based on Immune System

Dynamic Detection for Computer Virus Based on Immune System

The Tradition and Development of Dynamic Detection for Computer Virus Based on Immune System

3) Writing Requirements of a Good Title

Although the title comes first in a research paper, it may sometimes be composed last. Its final form may be long delayed and much thought about and argued over. In preparing a title, one salient fact must be remembered: That title will be read, as the first impression of a paper, by thousands of people. A successful title will attract readers while an unsuccessful one will discourage them. A good title is the fewest possible words that adequately describe the contents of the paper. Good academic paper titles require these:

* The title should indicate the topic of the study;

* The title should indicate the scope of the study (i.e., neither overstating nor understating its significance);

* The title should be self-explanatory to readers in the chosen area.

When presenting the writing requirements of a good academic paper title, six main problems are tackled in this section, concerning the length, word choice, question title, unity, capitalization and standard.[①]

(1) Length of the Title: Be Brief and Concise

Generally, a title is composed of no more than twenty words. If a title is too long, it would be difficult for readers to catch the meaning of the content and remember it. If you fail to state your idea clearly in a few words, you can use a subtitle.

---

① 张建, 陈赟. SCI/EI学术论文写作与发表攻略[M]. 北京: 机械工业出版社, 2018.

E.g. International Communication Pragmatics

—A New Branch of Learning of Language.

To be brief and concise, professional papers seldom use such decorative locutions as "on the..." "regarding..." ":investigations on..." "studies on..." "the method of..." "some thoughts on..." "a research of..." , which lead to redundancy. Of course, the title must be long enough to describe the content of the paper. Too short a title, sometimes, may bring about confusion.

(2) Word Choice: Be Specific

In preparing the title of an academic paper, a general and abstract title should be avoided. The title must be long enough to describe the content of the paper. While too short a title, sometimes, may bring about confusion or cannot indicate the subject and scope of a research paper with some accuracy. So, it should be specific and concrete.

(3) Be Not a Question Title

A question title means a complete sentence in the question form. Such titles are usually not used in an academic paper (especially in natural sciences) because they always include some redundant question words and marks, for example, "Is there...?" or "When does...?" or "Should the...?" or "Is it...?" If your title really contains a question, you may adopt the form of "question word + infinitive" , such as *Essential Steps for Writing a Title Page: How to Prepare the Title, Affiliation and Keywords.*

(4) Be Unified

In addition, a unified title is preferable in preparing a research paper title, that is to say, the parallel parts of a title should be grammatically symmetrical. That is to say, nouns should be matched with nouns, gerunds with gerunds, etc. In general, nouns and gerunds should not be mixed in a given title.

(5) Be Capitalized

There is not a single set of rules for capitalizing words in an academic paper title. Whether academic paper titles should be capitalized or not, may depend upon the specific requirements set forth by the journal to which your manuscript is to be submitted.

Types of Title	Writing Conventions for Capitalization of a Title	Example
Sentence Case / Down Style	Only the first word of the title and any proper nouns are capitalized	Rules for capitalizing the words in a title
Title Case / Heading Style / Up Style	Capitalize the first and last words of the title and all principal words, such as: nouns, adjectives, verbs, adverbs, pronouns, numerals, quantifiers	Rules for Capitalizing the Words in a Title
Fully Capitalizing	Capitalize all the words of a title	RULES FOR CAPITALIZING THE WORDS IN A TITLE

(6) Be Standard

In general, nonstandard abbreviations and symbols, and/or any terms or phraseology intelligible only to the specialist should be avoided.

4) Linguistic Features of a Good Title

Using more nouns, noun phrases and gerunds

The words or phrases used in a title are very often nouns, noun phrases or gerunds, nominalization, which are usually keywords for the paper, having the ability to sum up the whole text.

Using an incomplete sentence

Most academic paper titles are incomplete sentences. A title is just a label of the paper, reflecting the main idea of the contents, so even when there is a need to give a title in the form of a sentence, it does not need to be complete.

[Sample Analysis]

Title 1 *An Investigation of Mechanisms of Retinal（视网膜的）Damage from Chronic Laser Radiation*

Title 2 *A New Frequency Domain Speech Scrambling System Which Doesn't Require Frame Synchronization*

Title 3 *Network connectivity assessment and improvement through relay node deployment*

Title 4 *Effects of Acute Changes in Canine LV-Chamber Volume and Shape on Accuracy of Impedance Catheter Estimates of LV-Chamber Volume*

2.2 Author and Affiliation

2.2.1 General Functions

1) Bearing author's responsibility

Author and affiliation mainly help the authors respond to comments and questions given in their paper because they must perform the entire work of paper writing in person and be responsible for the content of the paper.

2) Facilitating retrieval and correspondence

The names of authors and institutional affiliations are usually used as author indexing. Readers can correspond with the authors according to the affiliation.

3) Heightening celebrity

Publication of a research paper is regarded as a norm for valuing the professional level of the researcher and the academic institution concerned.

2.2.2 Rules of Spelling a Name

Different journals or conferences are slightly different in the way they are signed. In most cases, for Chinese, a given name is put in the first place and a surname last with a space added in between. However, the situation is not completely exclusive. Several samples are advisable as follows:

* X.L. REN

* Xiaolian Ren

* XIAOLIAN REN

* Ren Xiaolian

* REN Xiaolian

2.2.3 Writing Requirements of Author and Affiliation

1) Printing format unified

It means that the format of author and affiliation should be uniformly printed in accordance with that of a Press.

2) Number of authors

In general, it is advised that the number of authors should not be over four. Too many authors listed may lead to inconvenience in author indexing. In case of real need, it is advisable to use "et al." after the principal authors. When authors' names are more than one, they should be separated with a comma. When several authors come from different affiliations, the serial number such as 1, 2, 3, etc. should appear in the up right corner of the authors' names. Different affiliations should be marked with the corresponding serial numbers and spaced by a semicolon.

3) Professional title omitted

The professional title, administrative rank or academic degree such as "Professor" "President" "Chief Manager" "PH.D", etc. are preferably omitted before the name of an author.

4) Affiliation

Affiliation refers to the organization to which the authors belong and where they work as a full-time job such as a university, a college, a school of a university, an institute, a bureau of a local government and so forth. Their affiliation is often described from the smaller unit to the larger one, just as those written on an envelope.

[Sample Analysis]

Guangxue Luo

School of Chemistry and Environmental Engineering,

China University of Mining and Technology, Beijing

Beijing 100083, P.R. China

Xiangyang Ma [1], Dongqing Liu [2]

(1. English Teaching Department of Shandong Normal University, Jinan Shandong

250014, China; 2. Foreign language Qingdao Agricultural University,

Qingdao Shandong 266109, China)

2.3 Keywords

1) General Functions

<u>Easiness of Retrieval</u>

Keywords of a research paper are the most frequently-used words and the most important words or phrases of the paper. As it mainly functions for easiness of retrieval, keywords are also called "indexing terms".

<u>Easiness of Highlighting</u>

Keywords are the most important words and phrases representative of the theme or subject matter of the paper.

2) Linguistic Features

<u>Nominalization</u>

Keywords are usually used in the form of nouns, not verbs. Keywords may be single words or word clusters.

<u>Limited Number</u>

The number of keywords for a paper should be limited. Three to five keywords are the average. In general, there should be at least 3 and at most 8.

<u>Designated Choice</u>

The keywords of a paper usually come from the title and/or the abstract, where the key words and phrases are usually contained.

3) Writing Requirements

<u>Placing in right location</u>

Though keywords can be either above or below the abstract of a paper, they are yet, in most cases, placed below the abstract.

<u>Spacing the keywords</u>

Use comma (,) or semicolon (;) to separate the words. Do not use full stop (.) after the last keyword.

Adopting standard abbreviations

Standard abbreviations are preferred in the section of keywords.

Reflections and Practice

I. Give your comments on the following titles and keywords or revise them if necessary.

1. Title

1) On Learning Foreign Languages and Cultural Background Teaching

2) A Research on the Artificial Neural Network (ANN) Applied in the Analysis of Structural Mechanics

3) JAX-WS enabled digital ecosystems approach for coal mining applications

4) A Visualization of the Relationship between Kirchhoff Migrating and Seismic Inversion

5) Inputting Cross-cultural Information for More Effective English Teaching by Means of Inputting Cross-cultural Communication in General College English Teaching

6) Is Literature Useless in GRE?

7) Artificial Intelligence and Pattern Recognition

8) Can the Rate of Wash Load Be Predicted from the Bed Load Function?

9) On the Communicative Skills —Advanced English Communication Course for Non-English Major Postgraduates in Tsinghua University

10) Model of environmental life cycle on how we assess coal mining operations

2. Keywords

1) Keywords: English, vocabulary, grammar, aptitude.

2) Keywords: Database, Deflector, Diffraction, Diaphragm

3) Keywords: information, Work Energy, Energy, Eco-energy, ecological law of thermodynamics

4) Keywords: bioremediation efficacy; mercury resistant; bacteria, HCG

5) Keywords: gas—solid fluidized bed

6) Keywords: idiom; comparison; differences; similarities; English; Chinese; customary usage; typical expression; essential meaning

Unit 3 Abstract

3.1 Definition of Abstract

An abstract is a brief summary of the most important points in a research paper. It is a concise summary of a larger project that concisely describes the content and scope of the project and identifies the project's objective, its methodology, findings, intended results and significances.

The abstract is usually placed before the introduction of a paper, but it is usually the last part of the paper to be written. All other sections of the paper should have been completed before the essential information can be selected and summarized.

3.2 General Functions of Abstract

1) Miniaturizing the Text

As a short, concise and highly generalized text, an abstract is viewed as a mini-version or a miniature of the document, summarizing the content of the main body. A well-prepared abstract, which serves as a useful tool in searching for information, enables readers to identify the basic content of a document more quickly and conveniently, to determine its relevance to their interest, and finally to decide whether they need to read the whole document.

2) Deciding "Yes" or "No"

The abstract of a paper is important because it may directly influence the paper's acceptance to a learned journal: the reviewer or editor may be very close to a final judgment of the manuscript after reading the abstract alone. A well-prepared abstract enables readers to identify the basic content of a document quickly and accurately, to determine its relevance to their interests, and thus to decide whether they need to read the document in its entirety or not.

3) Expanding the Circulation

An abstract usually precedes the whole paper and appears separately with the growth of electronic data storage, abstracts dramatically facilitate information retrieval.

3.3 Features of Abstract

1) Limited Length

An abstract is a miniature of the paper with a strictly limited number of words. Normally, 200 words should be a sensible maximum for a relatively long paper or report, but never more than 500 words; 50~100 words may suffice for a short article. The length of an abstract greatly varies depending on the length of the paper and where the abstract appears: each journal and/or abstracting index has a different requirement. As a general rule, an abstract will be approximately 3%~5% of the length of the paper, but is seldom more than 2/3 of a page. Keep the length of the abstract to a required percentage of that of the paper. [1]

2) Categories of Abstracts

Abstracts can be classified into three categories: descriptive, informative and structured abstract. Among these informative abstract is more widely used.

Descriptive abstract:

A descriptive abstract, also called indicative abstract or topic abstract, outlines the topics covered in a piece of writing so that the reader can decide whether to read the entire document. In many ways, the descriptive abstract is like a table of contents in paragraph form. It mainly introduces the point of view or research purposes of the paper rather than the research methods, findings, conclusions and recommendations. Descriptive abstracts are often used for theoretical papers, and they are short and

---

[1] 胡庚申. 英语论文写作与国际发表[M]. 北京: 外语教学与研究出版社, 2014.

terse, 100 words or less.

Informative abstract:

An informative abstract, as its name implies, summarizes the key points in the academic paper. It includes the information that can be found in a descriptive abstract (purpose, scope, methods) as well as the results and conclusions of the research and the recommendations of the author. An informative abstract, instead of indicating the whole content in general, should be specific and quantitative, and give only essential data. It highlights the findings and results without discussion or interpretation. It is particularly suitable for experimental studies. Most of academic journal articles use informative abstracts. The length varies according to discipline, but an informative abstract is rarely more than 10% of the length of the entire paper, and the word limit is in general between 150~250 words.

One of the strategies for writing an informative abstract is to go through the research paper with a highlighter and mark the important facts and conclusions. Another is to list the headings and write a sentence under each heading using key words for each area. Informative abstracts are written in a paragraph or two with transition words to signify the move between elements.

Structured abstract:

Sometimes, informative abstracts are divided into subheadings for each of these elements. These subheadings are written in full capitalization, bold face or italic face. These abstracts are called structured abstracts, appeared in the 1980s and are, by now, widely used in the major clinical journals. Many behavioral, social, biological, and basic medical sciences journals are also following the convention of structured abstracts. They will use headings such as: Objective, Design, Setting, Population, Participants (patients), Intervention (method) [①]

3) Complete Content

The abstract of a paper, which is self-contained, should be unified and coherent in content. It is a concise summary of the results, conclusion and/or other significant

---

① 李达, 李玉成, 李春艳. SCI论文写作解析[M]. 北京: 清华大学出版社, 2012.

items in the paper. An informative abstract, for instance, should at least contain the following five elements:

* Study context: background information;
* Purpose and scope: statement of the problem;
* Methodology: statement of the approach to solving the problem;
* Result: the most important results of the study;
* Conclusion: the significance or recommendation if necessary.

4) Formalized Structure

From the dimension of linguistic structure, a comparatively complete abstract usually consists of the following three major parts: topic sentence, supporting sentence, and concluding sentence.

(1) Topic Sentence

Some sentence patterns frequently used as topic sentences are listed as follows:

* The purpose of this paper is...
* The primary goal of this research is...
* The intention of this paper is to survey...
* The overall objective of this study is...
* The chief aim of the present work is to investigate the feature of...
* The authors are now initiating some experimental investigation to establish...
* The work presented in this paper focuses on several aspects of the following...
* The problem we have outlined deals largely with the study of...
* With his many years' research, the author's endeavor is to explain why...
* The primary object of this fundamental research will be to reveal the cause of...
* The main objective of our investigation has been to obtain some knowledge of...
* With recent research, the author intends to outline the framework of...
* The author attempts the set of experiments with a view to demonstrating certain phenomena...
* The experiment being made by our research group is aimed at obtaining the result of...

* Experiments on...are made in order to measure the amount of...

* The emphasis of this study lies in...

(2) Supporting Sentence

The topic sentence is usually followed by more than one supporting sentences which further specify the subject to be presented. Research methods, experiments, procedures, investigations, calculations, analysis, results, and other significant information items will be provided in this part. These supporting sentences, therefore, can be taken as the "main body" of an abstract.

Useful sentence patterns used in this part include the following:

* The method used in our study is known as...

* The technique we applied is referred to as...

* The procedure they followed can be briefly described as...

* The approach adopted extensively is called...

* Detailed information has been acquired by the authors using...

* The research has recorded valuable data using the newly-developed method.

* This is a working theory which is based on the idea that...

* The fundamental feature of this theory is as follows.

* The theory is characterized by...

* The experiment consisted of three steps, which are described in...

* The test equipment which was used consisted of...

* Included in the experiment are...

* The winch is composed of the following main parts...

* We have carried out several sets of experiments to test the validity of...

* They undertook many experiments to support the hypothesis which...

* Recent experiments in this area suggested that...

* A number of experiments were performed to check...

* Examples with actual experiment demonstrate...

* Special mention is given here to...

* This formula is verified by...

* We also supply...

(3) Concluding Sentence

As the ending part of an abstract, concluding sentences usually analyze the results, explain the application, and point out the significance of the research.

Some useful sentence patterns are listed below:

* In conclusion, we state that...

* In summing up it may be stated that...

* It is concluded that...

* The results of the experiment indicate that...

* The studies we have performed show that...

* The investigation carried out by... has revealed that...

* Laboratory studies of... did not furnish any information about...

* As a result of our experiments, we conclude that...

* From our experiment, the authors come to realize that...

* This fruitful work gives explanation of...

* The author's pioneer work has contributed to our present understanding of...

* The research work has brought about a discovery of...

* These research findings have led the author to the conclusion that...

* The data obtained appear to be very similar to those reported earlier by...

* Our work involving studies of... proves to be encouraging.

* The author has satisfactorily come to the conclusions that...

* Finally, a summary is given of...

3.4 Writing Requirements for Abstract

1) Integrity: to confine the abstract to a single paragraph with limited words and necessary elements of information.

2) Conciseness: to orient readers to a subject in an efficient manner using great economy of words. Expose the core of author's contribution and strip away the supporting information, defining the real substance of the manuscript in simplest

terms. Avoid displaying mathematical expressions, number equations and omit tables.

3) Consistency: to be consistent with the other parts of the whole paper, and never include what has not been mentioned in the paper.

4) Concentration: to omit such elements of information as figures, tables, or literature reviews in an abstract, to avoid repeating the unnecessary elements that conventionally appear in other sections of the paper.

5) Completeness: to include what have been done and achieved within the scope of the topic, such as the research theories, research methods, investigations, and results and conclusions, and to differentiate the present paper work from others by stressing this paper's contribution.[1]

3.5 "5 A Strategy" for Abstract Writing

Suppose you are asked to write an abstract for your research in no more than 150 words, make sure what you say is critical and objective for your potential readers. It will be easier for you to finish your abstract satisfactorily by answering the following five questions:

Q1: What is the general knowledge of your topic in the academic field?

Q2: What research topic is the paper to focus on?

Q3: What method or material do you use to support your main point of view?

Q4: What conclusion will you draw?

Q5: What is the main contribution of the paper?

Then the formula of writing an abstract is:

Abstract = A1 + A2 + A3 + A4 + A5

where, A1 to Q1 (one sentence or two sentences)

A2 to Q2 (one topic sentence, one or two supporting sentences that set forth the research topic if necessary)

A3 to Q3 (two or three sentences to give specific information about the research)

A4 to Q4 (one sentence)

---

[1] 马莉. 英语学术论文写作及语体风格[M]. 北京: 北京大学出版社, 2011.

A5 to Q5 (one sentence) ①

Let us take a look at the following example and see how the above formula works.

[Abstract]

(1) One of the most important problems in exploration seismology is to relate the surface seismic measurements with the subsurface geologic parameters. (2) The concept of wavefront curvature has been in extensive use for this purpose. (3) This paper extends the wavefront curvature concept to more general, transversely isotropic media. (4) After a brief discussion on ray tracing, a procedure is developed to describe the local properties of the ray based on an elliptical surface fit to the actual wave surface. (5) The apparent velocities of the elliptical fit are then used to generalize the seismic parameters developed in Byun (1982). (6) Simple numerical experiments are given to demonstrate the explorational significance of the theory. (7) It is shown that the measurements of the normal moveout velocity are not sufficient to estimate the velocity structure of the transversely isotropic medium. (8) The "sideslip" effect can lead to significant errors in depth mapping dipping reflectors.

In terms of the "5A strategy", the structure of the above abstract can be shown in the following table.

A1: background	Sentence 1, 2
A2: main topic	Sentence 3
A3: specific investigation	Sentence 4, 5, 6
A4: result and suggestion	Sentence 7
A5: conclusion and contribution	Sentence 8

3.6 Likely Mistakes and Common Errors in Abstract Writing

1) Mixed Writing Style

[Sample Abstract 1]

Multi-potential stem cells will be able to be separated from embryos or given

---

① 胡庚申. 英语论文写作与国际发表[M]. 北京: 外语教学与研究出版社, 2014.

by reprogramming. Pluripotency will be stabilized by an interconnected network of pluripotency genes that cooperatively regulate gene expression. Here we are committed to showing the molecular rules of pluripotency gene function and lay stress on post-transcriptional controls, particularly those induced by RNA-binding proteins and alternative splicing, like an important regulatory layer of pluripotency. In addition, I have confirmed the saying that heterogeneity in pluripotency regulation, alternative pluripotency states and future directions of pluripotent stem cell research.

[Sample Abstract 2]

My paper examines how selected research articles (RAs) reporting empirical investigations in applied linguistics proceed from first giving results to eventually giving final conclusions or some other form of closure. After going through the literature on a good many of relevant aspects of RA structure and its functions, I want to show the findings of a genre analysis of 20 RAs in applied linguistics concerning rhetorical choices among possible Results, Results and Discussion, Discussion, Conclusion, and Pedagogic Implications sections, and identify specific organizational choices within each section. I am convinced of a two-level account (Moves and Steps) of the separate Discussion sections in my corpus, and say this is able to catch general trends and specific rhetorical realizations in an insightful way.

Formal style and the colloquial style are mixed up in these two sample abstracts. Informal writing takes on the characteristics of a spoken conversation. It also takes on a personal tone whereby you speak directly to your audience. You can use first or third person point-of-view, and you're likely to address the reader using second person pronouns (e.g. you, your) . An informal writing style shows a level of familiarity and personality that sets it apart. Meanwhile, formal writing most often takes place on serious topics in a direct and succinct way, which is highly inclined in abstract writing.

2) Over-Simplified Statements

[Sample Abstract 3]

The domestic study status and problems of intrinsic safety in coalmine are analyzed; the connotation of intrinsic safety is further discussed.

3) Monotonous Expression

In writing an abstract, variety in the form is desired: long sentences should be alternatively used with short ones, so should be with passive and active voices, changing of verbs and phrases, and others. Lack of variety may lead to monotonous expression. Let us see the following examples:

[Sample Abstract 4]

GIS Spatial Analysis is widely adopted in the research of land use change, especially in the spatial research of land use change. The data analyzed by GIS is mainly from original land use map and remote sensing. Spatio-temperal data model, attribute data model and principal model for acquiring land use characteristics are included in the model foundation. Many functions of GIS, such as data conversion, edit function, spatial analysis, database operating, and statistic function are involved in the data dealing process. Taking Beijing area as an example, GIS spatial analysis and its application in the research of land use change are illustrated this paper.

All the five sentences in sample abstract 4 are in passive form. Lack of variety in voice factually leads to monotonous and stiff expression.

4) Incomplete contents

[Sample Abstract 5]

The viscoelastic property of various lubricating oils was measured with the oscillating crystal technique. The relation between the shear relaxation behavior and the molecular structure of the lubricating oils is discussed. Eyring's theory for viscous flow is used to explain the relaxation behavior from a molecular point of view. Some insight into a procedure for estimating the relaxation time from the molecular structure is presented.

Glancing at the above abstract, we may have an impression on it as follows:

First, in accordance with the requirements of abstract writing, the content of an abstract should be integrated or unified. But this abstract does not inform the readers of any result of the research.

Second, in terms of structure, the topic sentence of the abstract seems rather indistinctive, which creates difficulty for the reader to decide what the main objective of the paper is.

Third, the verb forms and sentence patterns used in it seem to be monotonous. All the four sentences in the abstract are in passive form.

Finally, some expressions in the abstract remain to be improved grammatically, such as "from a molecular point of view" "some insight into" , etc.

5) Displacement of information

[Sample Abstract 6]

The period of the1920s is the golden age of American literature. For Fitzgerald, who lived in the midst of the "roaring twenties" and was part of it all: driving fast cars, drinking hard whisky, and taking an immense delight in it, America was, he was perceptive enough to understand, "a moon that never rose" . As much as he enjoyed the "roaring" of the post war boom years, he foresaw its doom and failure. The Great Gatsby, his masterpiece, was produced in the background of the 1920s. The success of The Great Gatsby lies partly in the fact that it can be read in different ways. The story primarily concerns the young and mysterious millionaire Jay Gatsby and his quixotic passion and obsession for the beautiful former debutante Daisy Buchanan. It is possible to read it as a love story. On the other hand, the novel may be taken as a piece of social satire. The concern is with the corruption of values and the decline of spiritual life a condition which is related to the American dream. The essay focuses on that theme to illustrate the dream from its origin to its development and corruption.

The above abstract can be regarded as a poor version. The whole abstract consists of nine sentences, eight of which are used to present merely background information and general professional knowledge. Thus, the abstract does not provide any essential research information that should be provided in an abstract. Only the last sentence seems meaningful for an abstract.

Reflections and Practice

I. Analyze the abstracts below, following the direction stated below, if possible.

(1) categorize each abstract

(2) underline the topic sentence (s)

(3) circle the supporting sentences

(4) draw a box around the conclusion of each

[Abstract 1]

This report describes the practices and selected foreign countries for providing engineering expertise on shift in nuclear power plants. The report discusses the extent to which engineering expertise is made available and the alternative models of providing such expertise. The implications of foreign practices for U. S. consideration are discussed, with particular reference to the shift.

[Abstract 2]

The Wangjialing Mine in southern Shanxi Province is seriously threatened by roof water and is infamous for a water inrush disaster that happened there in 2010. The chief aim of the present work is to conduct a root-cause-analysis from three key issues, the height of the mining-induced fractured zone in formations overlying the coal seam, the water yield of aquifers (含) overlying the coal seam, and working face water inflows before and after pretreatment of roof water-bearing aquifers. According to the multi-source information composite principle, abundance zoning maps (区划图) of the roof aquifer were made using the overlapping function of geographic information system (GIS) for five controlling factors: aquifer thickness, total core recovery, drilling fluid quantity, permeability, and thickness of brittle and plastic strata (地层). Borehole (地上凿洞) -specific data from in-situ (现场,原位) pumping tests were used to verify the water abundance results. For areas that did not meet the verification requirements, the weights of the controlling factors were calibrated by reestablishing the analytic hierarchy process judgment matrix. The total height of the fractured zone within the #2 coal seam roof was calculated using an empirical formula. An established roof crack safety zoning map was used to evaluate that aspect. A three-dimensional numerical simulation of the groundwater flow system was established based on the site conceptual model of the roof aquifer and was used to predict the working face inflows. The results indicated that the 20,518 working face of the 205 panel had the greatest abundance of water.

[Abstract 3]

Objectives: To determine whether a computerized decision support system for initiation and control of oral anticoagulant improves quality of anticoagulant control achieved by trainee doctors

Design: Randomized control trial

Setting: District general hospital in North London

Subjects:148 inpatients requiring start of Warfarin (华法灵 / 苄丙酮香豆素) treatment

Interventions: Management by trainee doctors (to achieve therapeutic range of international normalized ration of 2 to 3) with indirect assistance from computerized decision support system (intervention group) or without such assistance (control group)

Main outcome measures: Median time to therapeutic range, stable dose, and first pseudo-event (excessive international normalized-spent in the therapeutic range

II. **Find an abstract you have written before, try to analyze its topic sentence, supporting sentence and concluding sentence.**

III. **Write specific sentences**

Each sentence below is a topic (general) sentence. Write a specific sentence that gives further information on the general sentence.

1. General: A wealth of information creates a poverty of attention.

Specific:

2. General: It is said that confidence is often the single ingredient that distinguish a successful person from someone less successful.

Specific:

3. General: My favorite season in Beijing is autumn.

Specific:

Unit 4 Introduction

4.1 Definition of Introduction

An introduction of a paper is to present background information that suggests why the topic is of interest. In other words, this section should contain: a description of the nature of the problem and current state of knowledge or understanding at the beginning of the investigation; a statement of the purpose, scope, and general method of investigation on the study.

4.2 General Functions of Introduction

Every academic paper should have at least one or two introductory paragraphs with or without a particular subtitle. The length or the degree of formality of a paper may decide whether the introduction should be a separate-labeled section.

1) Introducing the Subject

You are here to supply sufficient background information to relieve the readers who are not well-informed in this field of troubles and the results of the given study. Since the topic in this section is what the paper is going to deal with, the readers can get a preliminary but overall impression before going on with the full text of the paper. Do not get lost in reviewing background information. Remember that the introduction is meant to introduce the reader to the research, not summarize and evaluate all past literature on the subject (which is the purpose of a literature review.)

2) Limiting the Research Scope

Since there are so many perspectives to be dealt with and your research can proceed in any one of them, narrowing down the scope of work and delimiting the boundary of your study becomes entirely necessary.

The definition of scope may include the exact sphere of the general subject covered by the paper. The readers can be directed to a specific focus whether the work described is experimental or theoretical, etc.

Some functional devices are listed below:

* The problem is within the scope of...

* The problem under discussion is within the scope of...

* Studies of these effects covered various aspects of...

* Our studies with this technique are confined to only one particular aspect...

* The problem described previously was directed to the example of..., which differs from...

* This subject is concerned chiefly with the study of...

* The author has limited his studies to the related aspects of...

* The approach under study is only applied to...

* The problem I have referred to falls within the field of...

* The problem we have just outlined seems to be inside of the province of...

* The theory can not apply to other cases of...

3) Stating the General Purpose

If the first two functions of introduction, i.e. introducing the subject and limiting the research scope, are to usher the reader where to start and what to talk about in the paper, then the function of stating the general purpose is aimed at telling the reader why and where to start.

4) Showing the Writing Arrangement

The logical arrangement of the writing enables the reader to understand the paper more easily when further reading is necessary. The best place for this information can be found at the end of the introduction. Thus, a clear arrangement of your paper will make the reader feel convenient and active in their further reading.[1]

---

[1] 李芝. 英语学术论文写作教程[M]. 北京:中国人民大学出版社, 2017.

Some functional devices are listed below:

* This paper is divided into five major sections as follows
* Section one of this paper opens with...
* Section three develops the second hypotheses on...
* In this paper, data and results are presented under the major heading of...
* Section four shows (introduces, reveals, treats, develops, deals with etc.) ...

4.3 Structural Features of Introduction

1) Starting with the Research Background

The research background is usually given in the section of introduction accompanied by the recent development in this field. That is to answer the question, "What have been done? " Here are some expressions used to introduce the background of the subject in an introduction:

* Over the past several decades...
* Somebody reported...
* The previous work on...has indicated that...
* Recent experiments by...have suggested...
* Several researchers have theoretically investigated...
* In most studies of..., ...has been emphasized with attention being given to...
* Industrial use of... is becoming increasingly common.
* There have been a few studies highlighting...
* It is well known that...

2) Transiting to the Existing Problem

After the introduction of research background, it is necessary to transfer to the main problems to be discussed or weak points remaining in the previous work to be further studied and/or improved. That is to answer the question: "What have not been done? " The existing problems or weak points of such nature may be something that has not yet been found before, the methods that have not been adopted so far, materials that have not yet been discovered in the past, and/or the factors that were previously ignored, and so on.

The followings are a number of expressions used to present exiting problems:

* Great progress has been made in this field, but (however, nevertheless, etc,) ...
* Also, the consideration of... alone cannot explain the observed fact that...
* A part of the explanation could lie in... However...
* The study of... gives rise to two main difficulties: one is...; the other is...
* Despite the recent progress reviewed in..., there is no generally accepted theory concerning...
* From the above discussion, it appears that at present neither...nor...are known.
* A major problem...is the harmful effect exerted by...
* An experiment of this kind has not been made.
* The kind of experiment we have in mind has not been carried out until now.
* Until now no field experiments of...have been reported.
* Not any experiment in this area has suggested that...
* More than one experiment must be initiated to substantiate...
* The method we used differs greatly from the one reported ten years ago.
* The method of making...was not invented till the existence of...
* No clear advancement has so far been seen in...
* No direct outcome was then reported in...
* No such finding could be available in...
* So far there is not enough convincing evidence showing...
* The data available in literature failed to prove that...
* The theory of...did not explain how much modifications arose.

3) Focusing on the Present Research

On the basis of reviewing the previous research, especially unfolding or displaying the weak points of the previous work to be overcome or existing problems to be solved, you may gradually and naturally turn the reader's attention to the present research, by stating your primary research objectives, novel ideas, advanced methods, new materials, fresh factors, etc. that is to answer the question: "What am I going to do?" For example:

[Sample Introduction]

The aim of this paper can be divided into three parts.

Firstly, as we all know the anxiety exists in English learning of almost all the English learners, but how it exists and how much effect it brings to the learners are the questions which are unclear to us. This paper wants to find the answers to the questions through the result of the research questionnaire given to the non-English majors in China University of Mining and Technology, Beijing. This can also be called a step to collect the information about the subject.

Secondly, after collecting the information, this paper will make an analysis by using the collected information. This step which is the most important one can be called the analysis. Through this step, this paper will make up all the information, and then get the answers of the questions.

At last, this paper will give some advices after the analysis of the information. This is a step that can be called the solution. The research on anxiety of oral English is not a new area; there have already been some solutions to the problems, but the problems still exist. So, this paper tries again to find the exact reasons of why the English majors feel anxious when they speak English. Then, focusing on these reasons, this paper will give some practical suggestions to the learners.

There are also a number of expressions used to introduce the present work:

* In this paper, ...is investigated (studied, discussed, presented, etc.) ...
* The present work deals mainly with...
* We report here... in the presence of...
* This paper reports on...
* The present study will therefore focus on...
* The primary goal of this research is...
* The purpose of this paper (study, thesis, etc.) is...
* In this paper, we aim at...

4) Showing the Organization of the Paper

The following is a sample to present the organization of a thesis:

The thesis will be organized as follows:

Chapter 1 is an introduction of ... including research background, research significance and the organization of the thesis.

Chapter 2 is literature review, which introduces the theoretical foundation of ... It also contains overview of early studies on ... analyzing the advantages and shortcomings of previous studies and reasserts the opinions and significance in the present study.

Chapter 3 ...

Chapter 4 ...

Chapter5 draws a brief conclusion, reviews the significant contribution and makes a summary of the major findings.

Reflections and Practice

Analyze the following introductions, following the directions if possible.

1. Underline the part stating the research background.

2. Parenthesize the part pointing to the existing problem.

3. Draw a box around the part focusing on the present research.

[Introduction 1]

Alcoholic beverage, so-called wine, is a kind of drink with edible alcohol made of grain, fruit, leaf, seed, or other plants which are rich in sugar and starch. It is produced in the process of saccharification, fermentation, distillation, aging and other technologies by yeast micro-organisms' breakdown of sugar. We can see that in friends' meeting, wedding banquet, or for communication, business negotiation, alcoholic beverage almost penetrates into almost every family, deeply rooted in the human being's material life and spiritual life, and has a great influence and impact in it.

As a form of cultural representative, alcoholic beverage has become a part of material production and spiritual existence in man's life. It occurs on various occasions, for example, public or private interaction, festivals or daily meals. Many scholars have contributed a lot of efforts to conduct various researches on alcoholic beverage culture. Mostly their researches tend to be on a material level about ancient poetry, politics, and drinking etiquette. In a different way, this research will not only discuss these differences, but also analyze it in a cross-cultural perspective involving different Chinese and Western regions, values and so on, and then will find out the difference of Chinese and Western alcoholic beverage cultures is the difference of their cultural origins and values.

The purpose of this study is to make a comparison between Chinese and Western alcoholic beverage. Due to the differences of living environment, historical background, traditional custom, concept of value, thinking pattern and social norm, alcoholic beverage culture presents different style in China and the West. This study will provide the comparison of the two cultures in a material level, and then elaborate the factors involved which contribute to these differences. The study is not to judge which culture is better, but to explore the characteristics of different societies, to have an overall understanding of each culture, so as to learn from each other, avoid embarrassments and provide more experience for people to make cross-cultural communication today.

[Introduction 2]

With the development of globalization and increasing popularity of English in China, good oral English is highly valued. Some people even regard better pronunciation as the symbol of better English. What's more, correct pronunciation is vital for the acquisition of vocabulary and grammar as well as for the improvement of listening, speaking, reading, writing and translating abilities. However, since every language has its phonetic system, most Chinese learners are accustomed to the manner of articulating Chinese speech sounds. When learning the English pronunciation, they have many difficulties in imitating English sounds. It is well known that there are different dialects in Chinese. Therefore, learners' difficulties in pronunciation vary from region to region. According to the most popular classification, Chinese dialects can be divided into seven major dialects. One of them is Xiang dialect.

In Hunan province, college students have learned English at least for 6 or 9 years, but such a long period does not guarantee standard pronunciation. Many people fail to identify and correct the phonetic problems when they begin to learn Putonghua, not to mention English. This ignorance usually causes misperception. Misperception precedes mispronunciation and inhibits the development of listening, which in turn affects the vocabulary learning and reading and other language skills. Thus, it is necessary to identify their phonetic problems. It is sharply pointed out by Fraser that "pronunciation skills often correlated poorly with general language skills" (2001:50). Students can get advanced in grammar, vocabulary and literary skills but remain beginners in pronunciation. For this reason, pronunciation should be again emphasized. Some college students majoring in English are the would-be teachers. If they carry the pronunciation problem, they will pass it on to the following generations. "A good grounding in basic pronunciation is a valuable gift that any ESL (English as a Second Language) teacher can give to any learner" (ibid: 51).

This study makes a contrastive analysis on English word pronunciation between the standard pronunciation and pronunciation affected by Xiang dialect, using the software Praat to cut and visualize the sound, supplemented with data from questionnaires. It is hoped that the result could scientifically identify the phonetic problems, provide the learners with some implications and guidance and give the teachers more statistics for reference, thus helping improve the teaching of English pronunciation in the future.

Unit 5 Literature Review

5.1 Definition of Literature Review

For those new to academic research, the literature review is one of the least understood parts of a research project. A literature review is an overview of previous research on a topic. It can be either a part of a larger report of a research project, or a bibliographic essay published separately in a scholarly journal. Either way, the purpose is the same, to review the scholarly literature relevant to the topic that you are studying. This review will help you design your methodology and help others to interpret your research. Some questions you may think about as you develop your literature review are:

* What is known about the subject?

* Are there any gaps in the knowledge of the subject?

* Have areas of further study been identified by other researchers that you may want to consider?

* Who are the significant research personalities in this area?

* Is there consensus about the topic?

* What aspects have generated significant debate on the topic?

* What methods or problems were identified by others studying in the field and how might they impact your research?

* What is the most productive methodology for your research based on the literature you have reviewed?

* What is the current status of research in this area?

* What sources of information or data were identified that might be useful to you?

If the literature review is part of a Ph.D. thesis, this review will be comprehensive covering all research on the topic. As part of your research report, you will want to cover the major work that has been done on the topic recently, but it is not necessary to try to identify all research on the subject.

A literature review is a survey and discussion of the literature in a given area of study. It is a concise overview of what has been studied, argued, and established about a topic, and it is usually organized chronologically or thematically. A literature review is written in essay format. It is not an annotated bibliography, because it groups related works together and discusses trends and developments rather than focusing on one item at a time. It is not summary; it evaluates previous and current research in regard to how relevant and/or useful it is and how it relates to your own research. According to Creswell (2005), a literature review "is a critical summary and assessment of journal articles, books and other documents that describes the past and current state of information in a particular field". It more often is part of a research paper, constructed as an independent section.[①]

There are two main approaches to literature review writing. One approach is to choose an area of research, read all the relevant studies, and organize them in a meaningful way. Another is to choose an organizing theme or a point that you want to make, and then select your studies accordingly.

It is a norm that any good literature review should include proper citations or referencing of ideas and quoted information with the intention of appreciating and providing a critique of what others have done in the same field of study. This is the most technical bit of literature review.

5.2 Purpose of Literature Review

The literature review in a an academic paper is part of the secondary research and its purposes include: to show what has been previously studied in the field

---

① 张建, 陈赟. SCI/EI学术论文写作与发表攻略[M]. 北京: 机械工业出版社, 2018.

and what can be improved or modified; to summarize other people's writings; to define or review definitions and key concepts, and to clear the ground for your own research. If you are familiar with previous studies in the field, you are likely to see the gaps that need to be filled and opportunities for further studies to be undertaken. Consequently, this is the starting point of your research. If you are unable to provide a good review of the literature, this implies that you are not familiar with the research situation or that you are not able to summarize other people's research in this area.

In writing a literature review, our goal is to convey to our readers what knowledge and ideas have been established on a topic, and what their strengths and weakness are, that's to say, a literature review contains two basic elements: to thoroughly describe the work done in a specific area of research and to evaluate this work. Both the descriptive and evaluative elements are important parts of the review. We cannot do one or the other. If we just describe past research without evaluating it, we are merely summarizing information without digesting it. If we just discuss recent theories in an area without describing the work done to test those theories, our arguments will lack supporting empirical evidence.

By highlighting these arguments, the writer attempts to show what has been studied in the field, and also where the weaknesses, gaps, or areas needing further study are. The review should therefore also demonstrate to readers why the writer's research is useful, necessary, important, and valid.

The literature review section is where the tutor can assess whether the student has done enough reading of the relevant studies in the field and whether the student is familiar with the research background and situation.

5.3 Format of Organizing a Literature Review

There are many formats to organize a literature review. Three of the most common are the chronological format, the thematic format, and the methodological format.

Chronological:

In historical format the review is chronologically organized. We will group and discuss our sources in order of their appearance (usually publication) highlighting the changes in research in the field and our specific topic over time. This format is useful for papers focusing on research methodology, historiographical papers, and other writings where time becomes an important element. It is preferred when the emphasis is on the progression of research methods or theories or on a change in practices over time.

Thematic:

A second common organizational scheme is built around concepts. In conceptual format, we will group and discuss our sources in terms of the themes or topics they cover. This format is often a stronger one organizationally. It can help us resist the urge to summarize our sources. By grouping themes or topics of research together, you will be able to demonstrate the types of topics that are important to our research.

Methodological:

A methodological approach differs from the two above in that the focusing factor usually does not have to do with the content of the material. Instead, it focuses on the "methods" of the researcher or writer. In methodological format, research methods in the chosen field are investigated to identify key variables, measures, and methods of analysis. The methodological review is also helpful to identify methodological strengths and weaknesses in a body of research, and examine how research practices differ across groups, times, or settings. A methodological review may lead to sound rationale that can justify proposed research.[①]

Within each section of a literature review, it is important to discuss how the research relates to other studies (how it is similar or different, what other studies have been done, etc.) as well as to demonstrate how it relates to your own work. This is what the review is for: don't leave this connection out.

5.4 Content of a Literature Review

No matter how you decide to organize your literature review, it will have two

---

① 龚 杰. 英语学术论文高级写作技巧和发表指南[M]. 成都: 四川大学出版社, 2017.

purposes: to thoroughly describe the work done in a specific area of research, and to evaluate this work. In doing so, you may approach or structure your review from the chronological or theoretical to the empirical or from the general to the specific.

To achieve this goal, you need to write your review as clear and objective as you can. Discuss the least-related references to your question first and the most related reference last. In doing so, you may approach or structure your review from chronological or from the theoretical to the empirical, or from the general to the specific.

When you write a literature review, the major review focuses should be:

1) definitions of **key terms or concepts** relevant to your topic,

2) the prevailing and current **theories** which underlie the research problem,

3) the major **findings** in the area, by whom, and when,

4) the main **controversies** or **criticism** of the work in the area,

5) a brief **summary** to conclude relevant review,

6) the **rationale and purpose of the proposed study**.

5.5 Classification of Source Materials

In a library or bookstore, you can find a sea of books and journals. In order to locate the materials relevant to your topics better and faster, you should know about the kinds of your sources. Basically, all these source materials may be classified into three major kinds:

1) Background Sources

Background information can usually be found in dictionaries and encyclopedia complied by major scholars or founders of the field. Three very good and commonly-used encyclopedias are encyclopedia ABC, namely, Encyclopedia Americana, Encyclopedia Britannica, and Collier's Encyclopedia. Moreover, you may also find encyclopedias on the web.

2) Primary Sources

Primary sources are those providing direct evidence, such as works of scholars of the field, biographies or autobiographies, memoirs, speeches, lectures, diaries, collection of letters, interviews, case studies, approaches, etc. They come in various shapes and sizes, and often you have to do a little bit of research about the source to make sure you have correctly identified it. When a first search yields too few results, try searching by a broader topic; when a search yields too many results, refine your search by narrowing down your search.

3) Secondary Sources

Secondary Sources refer to those providing indirect evidence, such as research articles, research papers, book reviews, essays, journal articles by experts in a given field, studies on authors or writers and their works, etc. They will inform most of your writing in college. You will often be asked to research your topic using primary sources, but secondary sources will tell you which primary sources you should use and help you interpret those primary sources. To use them well, however, you need to think critically. There are two parts of a source that you need to analyze: the text itself and the argument within the text.[①]

5.6 Evaluating Source Materials in Literature Review

Reviewing literature is a process of researching. It is wrong and impossible to try to collect all the materials that have something to do with what you are writing. You should scan the sources on your working bibliography to evaluate which one you will use in writing your paper. The most important criterion for selecting a source is its relevance to your research plan. And you should be careful with the following guidelines.

1) Choose the Original or First-hand Materials

If you have several sources, one of them focusing on the work itself, while

---

① 姜秋霞. 研究生英语学术论文写作基础[M]. 上海: 复旦大学出版社, 2016.

others summarizing or explaining the work, choose the former one. Never intend to write about a topic without referring to the original work. No secondary work is going to give you the "facts". Secondary sources provide interpretations of primary data. Every interpretation is influenced by the author's context. Find out where the author is coming from and use the evidence accordingly.

2) Choose the Sources That Cover the Topic in Depth

Very often, you will find a number of sources on your target subject. However, few sources cover the topic in depth. Choose those important and typical materials to help your paper hold water. Check out the Book Review Index in the Reference section of the library. Read what other scholars have written about this book. And consider the following questions:

Are the reviews generally positive?

Do they consider the book useful or important to the field?

3) Choose Sources That State Different Viewpoints on Your Thesis

Take into account these arguments which demonstrate knowledge and consideration of other viewpoints and research in the field. Not only collect materials that support your arguments, but also collect the materials that don't support your arguments. Only in this way can your writing be proved scientific, and your arguments hold water.

4) Choose Up-to-date Materials

Make sure that your materials are current in terms of both its publication date and its information. Remember that knowledge changes more rapidly in some fields than in others. If you are researching a current issue, it stands to reason that you want the most up-to-date sources that you can find. If your topic is not so current, it is often acceptable to go back ten or even twenty years for your sources.

5) Choose the Most Authoritative Source

Try to find out whether the material is written by a reliable authority whose methods and reasoning appear valid. You may check the author's education or experience with the topic, and reputation should play a major part in your evaluation and use of a work.[①]

5.7 Language Focus: Citing Sources

There are two ways in which you can refer to, or cite, another person's work: by reporting or by direct quotation. Reporting means simply reporting other writers' ideas in your own words. You can either paraphrase if you want to keep the same length or summarize if you want to make the text shorter. There are two main ways of showing that you have used other writers' ideas: reporting and non-reporting, which are distinguished according to whether or not the name of the cited author occurs in the citing sentence or parenthesis.

Reporting	Integral	➢ Brie (2006) noted (found, reported, noted, suggested, observed, and pointed out) that the water boils at 100℃. ➢ Researchers such as Brie (2006), Aleanoni (2005) and Seldin (2007) have shown that the causes of illiteracy are complex.
	Non-integral	➢ As researchers have demonstrated, the procedure is harmful (Raimes, 2001; Zamel, 2003).
Non-reporting	Integral	➢ According to Peters (1983), evidence from first language acquisition indicates that lexical-phrases are learnt first as unanalyzed lexical chunks. The causes of illiteracy were investigated by Johnes (1987).
	Non-integral	➢ Lexical phrases are learnt first as unanalyzed non-lexical chunks (Peters, 1983). ➢ Several researchers have studied the causes of illiteracy.

As the above examples illustrate, there are three tense options: present indefinite, past indefinite, and present perfect. The differences among these tenses are subtle. In general, a move from past to present perfect and then to present indicates that the research reported is increasingly close to the author in some way: close to the author's own opinion, close to the author's own research, or close to the current

---

① 高霄. 学术英语论文写作[M]. 北京: 外语教学与研究出版社, 2015.

state of knowledge. The present tense choice is sometimes called the citational present and is also used with famous or important sources. For example, Plato argues that ... Confucius says ...[①]

In order to refer to the research of others or to report on their findings, you have to use reporting verbs just as Evans (1994) suggests that... Brown (2001) argues that ... The difficulty with using reporting verbs is that there are different verbs, and each of them has slightly different and often subtle meanings.

Using the correct words relies on making the correct interpretation of what the author you are studying is saying. The main reporting verbs in English may be classified in terms of their function and strength. Some reporting verbs are used principally to say what the author does and does not do. These verbs do not indicate any value judgment on the part of the author; they are called "neutral" reporting verbs. A second group of verbs is used to show when the author has an inclination to believe something but still wishes to be hesitant; we call these "tentative" reporting verbs. Finally, if the author has strong arguments to put forward and is absolutely sure of his or her ground, we can use "strong" reporting verbs to refer to these ideas.[②]

Function and Strength	Example Verbs
Neutral reporting verbs	Describe, show, reveal, study, demonstrate, note, point out, indicate, report, observe, assume, examine, state, etc.
Tentative reporting verbs	Suggest, speculate, intimate, hypothesize, imply, propose, recommend, postulate, etc.
Strong reporting verbs	Argue, claim, emphasize, contend, maintain, assert, theorize, support the view that, deny, negate, refute, reject, challenge, strongly believe that, counter the view that, etc.

---

① 吴江梅, 黄佩娟. 英语科技论文写作[M]. 北京: 中国人民大学出版社, 2013.
② 彭金定, 赵培玲. 学术论文写作实用指南[M]. 长沙: 中南大学出版社, 2015.

Unit 6 Result, Discussion and Conclusion

6.1 Section of Results

1) General Functions and Contents of Results

The value of a research lies in the value of its final results and the author's interpretation of the results. If the preceding sections of a paper (Introduction, Investigation, Experiments, Calculations, etc.) are designed to explain how you obtain the results, and the following sections of the paper (Analysis, Discussion, Summary or Conclusion, etc.) are to tell what the results should mean. Then, the section of results should bring about a solid foundation on which the whole paper rests, by boiling down all the facts and data you have gained.

In terms of content, research results are usually presented together with the corresponding analysis concerned. So, in this section you should present the essential results and data and then generalize them to a theoretical height. Therefore, there are usually two ingredients in this section: full presentation of the specific data of the work and detailed analysis of the results (esp. when there is no special section of Data Analysis in the paper).[1]

2) Writing Requirements for Results

First, any data shown in this section must be meaningful, so sorting out and selecting data should be highly necessary. Just as Dr. Jolin Powell, a noted American

---

[1] 李向武. 英语学术论文写作教程[M]. 成都: 西南交通大学出版社, 2014.

geologist, says, "The fool collects facts; the wise man selects them." Tables generally should report summary-level data, rather than all your raw data.

Second, A few concise, easy-to-read tables or figures bring out the main findings of your study. Number tables and figures separately beginning with 1 (i.e. Table 1, Table 2, Figure 1, etc.). Data may be presented in figures and tables, but this may not substitute for a verbal summary of the findings. The text should be understandable by someone who has not seen the figures and tables.

Third, the function of this section is to summarize general trends in the data without comment, bias or interpretation. Do not attempt to evaluate the results in this section. Report only what you have found; hold all discussion of the significance of the results for the Discussion section.

Although the presentation of result is the most important part of a paper, it is often the shortest section, particularly if it is preceded by a well-written part of Experiment or Materials and Methods, and followed by a well-written part of Analysis, Discussion, Summary or Conclusion. Sometimes, the result may possibly have just one sentence: "The results are shown in Table 1 (or Figure 1)". Of course, not all sections of result are as short as such.

3) Examples and Some Useful Expressions

Listed below are some useful expressions frequently encountered in the section of result.

* The research we have done suggests an increase in…

* As a result of our experiments, we concluded that…

* This fruitful work gives an explanation of…

* Our experimental data are briefly summarized as follows…

* Figure 3 shows the results obtained from studies of…

* Table 5 presents the data provided by the experiments on…

* This table summarized the data collected during the experiment of…

* Some of the author's findings are listed in tables.

* The direct outcome was then reported in…

* Sufficient result for... has been observed with the new method...

* This work did provide...

* Most recent experiments to the same effect have led the authors to believe that...

* As a result of our experiments, we concluded that...

6.2 Section of Discussion

1) General Functions and Main Elements of Discussion

If the function of result section is to show the facts observed by the researcher, then the purpose of discussion section is to expound the interrelations among the observed facts. Therefore, the primary objective in writing this section is to show the relationship between the facts, their underlying causes, their effect, and their theoretical implications, as well as to explain the facts denoted by symbols or signs of mathematics.

* Analyzing the Data

* Pointing Out Doubts

* Expounding Viewpoints

* Stating the Significance

* Arriving at a Conclusion

2) Writing Requirements for Discussion

Firstly, you should sufficiently analyze the presented data and point out the factual relationships.

Secondly, since the purpose of the academic paper is to confirm your research work, it is beneficial for you to fully review what you have done in your work. That means you have to fully evaluate your own success rather than just make a summary of facts.

Thirdly, brief and forceful expressions should be used in the section of discussion. End the discussion with a summary of the principle points that you want the reader to remember.

3) Common mistakes in Discussion Section

* Combined with results: The results and discussion sections cannot be combined. They have two very different purposes. The results section is for fact; the discussion section is for interpretation.

* Including new results: Sometimes a new result not reported in the Results section will be included in the discussion section, which is inappropriate.

* The "inconclusive": Don't waste time with a statement like "The results are inconclusive" or "The results are not consented" ①

6.3 Section of Conclusion

1) General Functions and Main Elements of Conclusion

Summing up

Summing up is likely to be a part with its main function of summarizing the chief pieces of pure facts, data and information in the paper, where formal conclusions or recommendations usually have no place. If you include a summary, make certain that you actually summarize, with due emphasis, the principal items of information in the main body of the paper, and that you include only material that appeared earlier in an expanded form.

Statements of Conclusions

Conclusions are convictions based on evidence. If you state conclusions, make certain that they follow logically from the data presented actually in the main body of the paper, and that they agree with whatever you may have promised to testify in the introduction.

Statement of Recommendations

Recommendations, at least formal ones, appear less frequently in academic papers than technical reports. If you include recommendations, be sure that they

---

① 陈新仁. 英语学术论文写作实用教程[M]. 苏州: 苏州大学出版社, 2012.

follow logically from the data and conclusions presented earlier, and do not dangle as proposals that you think are good but for which you have given no supporting evidence, and that, as with conclusions, they should never clash with what you may have expected to do in your introduction.

Graceful Termination

Graceful termination is achieved when all the materials of the conclusion are smoothly woven together and satisfactorily round off the whole.[1]

2) Requirements for Writing a Conclusion

*To make an effective contrast or comparison of the present results with the original hypothesis or assumption.

* Be careful not to draw conclusions from data with errors.

* No new material is introduced.

* Avoid confusing facts with opinions of influences, not only in the investigation itself but also in preparing results for publication.

* Give a sense of completeness or closure by alluding to instead of reciting the obvious.

3) Useful Expressions in Writing Conclusions

* On the basis of..., the following conclusion can be made...

* From..., we now conclude...

* To sum up, we have revealed...

* We have demonstrated in this paper...

* The results of the experiment indicate...

* In conclusion, the result shows...

* We have described..., and we found...

* Our argument proceeds in...

* The research work has brought about a discovery of...

* Finally, a summary is given of...

---

[1] 胡庚申. 英语论文写作与国际发表[M]. 北京: 外语教学与研究出版社, 2014.

*These findings of the research have led the author to the conclusion that...

*The research has resulted in a solution of...

*It can be concluded from...

Reflections and Practice

Find a research paper, try to analyze and revise its conclusion.

Unit 7 Preparing Oral Presentation

7.1 How to Prepare and Organize Your Oral Presentation

Before the presentation, you should think about two things: your audience and purpose. What is your audience's academic background and interest? Are they familiar with your topic and the special terms you might use? How are you going to involve them in your presentation? Why do you want to make your presentation? Do you want to inform your audience or inspire them to think about your topic or convince them of a particular point of view?

When drafting your presentation, you need summarize your draft into points to write on slides of PPT. Remember, you have a limited time for your presentation and should stick to your assigned time.

When rehearsing your presentation, you'd better ask a friend, a partner or a teacher to listen to, correct and time for you.

Like an essay, a presentation also has three main parts and follows this simple formula:

1) Tell the audience what you are going to say! = introduction
2) Say it! =Main part
3) Tell them what you said! =Conclusion

7.2 How to Open Your Presentation

Starter: Read the opening sentences of the two presentations and complete the table below (Grussendorf, 2007: 66):

[Presentation 1]

OK, shall we get started? Hello everyone. For those of you who don't know me, I'm Charlotte Best from IT. I'm a team leader. I'm happy that so many of you could make it today at such short notice. I know that you're all extremely busy at the moment, so I'd like to start with my presentation right away. As you can see on the screen, our topic today is project documentation. We're going to look closely at drafting, storing, archiving as well as accessing documents in our new SAP system. We'll also examine the much improved handling of all project documentation as well as user rights. This is extremely important for all of us who are directly involved in international project management, right? You don't need me to spell it out... if it isn't documented, it doesn't exist.

[Presentation 2]

Good afternoon. I'm aware that you all have very tight schedules, so I appreciate you taking the time to come here today. As you probably know, my name is Susan Webster. I'm the new human resources manager here at Weston Ltd. What I'd like to present to you today is my department's new concept for improving our in-company training and qualification programmes. This is based on feedback from your departments. Today's topic will be very important for you as department heads, since I'll need your help to evaluate and select candidates for training.

	Presentation 1	Presentation 2
Presenter's name		
Presenter's position/function		
Topic of presentation		
Who is the presentation for		

Question: Which presentation is formal and which less formal? Why?

1) Structure and Expressions for Your Presentation

Structure focus: Welcome the audience → Introduce yourself → Say what the topic is → Explain why audience will be interested → Give your agenda → The final part of the introduction

(1) Welcoming the Audience

* Hello/Hi, everyone.

* Good morning/afternoon, ladies and gentlemen.

* First of all, let me thank you all for coming here today.

* I'm happy/delighted that so many of you could make it today.

* I would like to start by thanking... for inviting me to be part of this (panel).

* I am honored to address you on the important occasion of...

* Thank you for that warm introduction. It is a great pleasure to be here with you today.

* I thank you for giving me this opportunity to share with you (some of my thoughts) and principally to learn quite a lot by being here.

(2) Introducing Yourself and Your Affiliation

* Let me introduce myself. I'm... from...

* As you probably know, I'm...

* For those of you who don't know me, my name is...

* I'm here in my function as the Head of Controlling.

* I am a Ph.D student/researcher/ technician at...

* I am doing a Ph.D/a Master/some research at...

* I am part of a team of 20 researchers and most of our funding comes from...

* The work that I am going to present to you today was carried out with the collaboration of the University of...

* Good morning. Let me start by saying just a few words about my own background/ myself.

(3) Saying What the Topic Is

* As you can see on the screen, our topic today is...

* Today's topic is...

* What I'd like to present to you today is...

* The subject of my presentation is...

* I am here to talk about a new way to select candidates for a position in a

company.

* My idea today is not to debate whether there's such a thing as good TV or bad TV; my idea today is to tell you that I believe television has a conscience.

* So I'm going to talk to you about the political chemistry of oil spills and why this is an incredibly important, long, oily, hot summer.

* I want to start my talk today with two observations about the human species and why we need to keep ourselves from getting distracted.

* I'd like to share with you a discovery that I made a few months ago while writing an article for Italian Wired.

* I'm speaking to you about what I call the "mesh". It's essentially a fundamental shift in our relationship with stuff, with the things in our lives.

* In this presentation I am going to/ would like to/I will discuss some findings of an international project.

* It is a pleasure for me to be here this afternoon and to address you on the subject of...

(4) Explaining What Point Your Research Has Reached and Why Audience Will Be Interested in

* My/The topic is very important for you because...

* By the end of this talk you will be familiar with...

* My talk is particular relevant to those of you /us who...

* Today's topic is of particular interest to those of you/us who...

* What I am going to present is actually still only in its early stages, but I really think that our findings so far are worth telling you.

* We are already at a quite advanced stage of the research but I was hoping to get some feedback from you on certain aspects relating to...

* Our research, which we have just finished, is actually part of a wider project involving...

(5) Giving the Agenda

* I will begin with an introduction to... / will begin by giving you an overview of...

Then I will move on to... After that I will deal with... And I will conclude with...

* First, I'd like to do X/ I'm going to do X/First, I'll be looking at X. Then we'll be looking at Y/Then, we'll focus on Y. And finally we'll have a look at Z. /Finally, I'm going to take you through Z. So, let's begin by looking at X.

* I have two missions here today. The first is to tell you something about pollen, I hope, and to convince you that it's more than just something that gets up your nose. And, secondly, to convince you that every home really ought to have a scanning electron microscope.

(6) The Final Part of the Introduction:

This section will tell the audience how long your presentation will last, whether there will be handouts, and how questions will be handled.

<u>Timing</u>

*My presentation will take about 20 minutes.

* It should take about 30 minutes to cover these issues.

<u>Handouts</u>

* Does everybody have a handout, brochure/report? Please take one, and pass them on.

* Don't worry about taking notes. I've put all the important statistics on a handout for you.

* I'll be handing out copies of the PowerPoint slides at the end of my talk.

* I'll email the PowerPoint presentation to you.

<u>Questions</u>

* There will be time for questions after my presentation.

* If you have any questions, feel free to interrupt me at any time.

* Feel free to ask questions at any time during my talk.

2) Language Focus

Here are a few techniques you can use to start your talk:

(1) Remember to Use Words like *We*, *Us*, and *Our* to Highlight Common Interest.

Experts say that the first few minutes of a presentation are the most important.

If you are able to get the audience's attention quickly, they will be interested in what you will say.

(2) Ask a Rhetorical Question

* Are exhaust emissions from vehicles a big factor in city haze?

* Will biofuel cause malnutrition in the world?

(3) Start with an Interesting or Controversial Fact

As we know, the incident at the Fukushima Daiichi nuclear power plant—a result of a devastating earthquake and subsequent tsunami on 11 march 2011—has re-invigorate the debate on how to meet the world's growing demands for energy and the contribution of nuclear power to the global energy mix.

(4) Tell Them a Story or Anecdote

* I remember when I attend a meeting in Paris...

* At a conference in Madrid, I was once asked the following question...

(5) Give Them a Problem to Think About

* Suppose you wanted to choose an environmentally friendly lifestyle, what would it be?

* Imagine you had to do something to reduce GHE. What would be your first step?

The purpose of the introduction is not only to tell the audience who you are, what the talk is about, and why it is relevant to them; you also want to tell the audience briefly how the talk is structured. Here are some useful phrases to talk about the structure.

* I've divided my presentation into three main parts: X, Y, and Z.

* In my presentation I'll focus on three major issues.

* First of all, I'll be looking at..., second..., and third...

* Then/next,...After that, I'll go on to...

* Finally, I'll offer some solutions.

Reflections and Practice (1)

Think of a presentation you have given or would like to give and use the checklist to prepare your introduction. Try to use phrases from this unit.

Checklist for introductions:

* Welcome the audience.

* Introduce yourself (name, position/function).

* State your topic.

* Explain why your topic is important for the audience.

* Outline the structure of your talk.

* "What comes then?" say when you'll be dealing with each point.

* Let the audience know how you're organizing the presentation (handouts, questions, etc.)

7.3 How to Deliver the Main Part of Your Presentation

Starter: Do this quiz about body language. Sometimes more than one answer is possible (Grussendorf, 2007: 15).

YOU'RE GIVING A PRESENTATION ...

1 How should you stand?
   a Arms crossed on chest.
   b Straight but relaxed.
   c Knees unlocked.

2 What should you do with your hands?
   a Put hands on hips.
   b Put one hand in a pocket.
   c Keep hands by your side.

3 How can you emphasize something?
   a Point finger at the audience.
   b Move or lean forward to show that something is important.
   c Use a pointer to draw attention to important facts.

4 What should you do when you feel nervous?
   a Hold a pen or cards in your hands.
   b Walk back and forth.
   c Look at the flip chart or screen (not at the audience).

5 How should you keep eye contact with the audience?
   a Make eye contact with each individual often.
   b Choose some individuals and look at them as often as possible.
   c Spread attention around the audience.

6 How fast should you speak?
   a About 20% more slowly than normal.
   b Just as fast as in a normal conversation.
   c Faster than in a normal conversation.

7 How should you express enthusiasm?
   a By raising voice level.
   b By waving arms.
   c By making hand or arm gestures for important points.

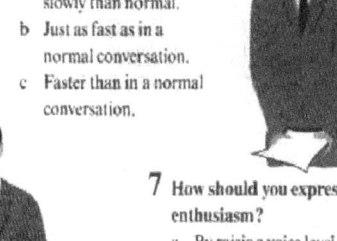

7.3.1 Structure Focus

1) Literature Review

(1) Overview the Subject, Issue or Theory (present simple tense/past simple tense/ present perfect tense)

* Previous investigations have attempted to predict heat loss and…

* Previous research has analyzed price promotions in a framework of one or more sellers who…

* Much importance has been placed on urban public transportation as a result of…

* There has been considerable research on the transfer of skills by labor migrants, especially within…

* There is a considerable body of research suggesting that through intercultural contact, cultures may increasingly become more homogeneous.

* Various authors studied the chemistry of phosphorus compounds in aqueous solutions.

* Most work was done in the 60s and 70s as a theoretical support for chemical precipitation of phosphorous compounds.

* The past 10 years have witnessed a growing interest amongst both academics and policy-makers in the relationship between trade and poverty.

* The study of knowledge labor and the information society has raised numerous important questions for academics and policy makers.

* Studies of language and identity have traditionally focused on how individuals or group maintain, construct, project or negotiate their and social identities in and through linguistic practices.

(2) Division of Work under Review into Categories (present simple tense/ past simple tense)

* Overall, studies conducted so far provide evidence that…

* Past studies in the optimum design of transit services can be reviewed with

regard to four aspects.

* As Buch et al. (1992) suggested earlier, shy students may drink less than peers with similar beliefs about the effects of alcohol on the self-regulation of behavior.

* The trade-growth-poverty relationship involves two critical linkages that have been at the center of heated debate during the past 10 years.

* Following-up on these studies, Green (1998) also reported that dysphonic students who had to wait in an unconstrained situation…

* The productivity crisis in the United States and the rest of the world has been well documented.

* As for the growth poverty linkage, many studies show that in the long run, growth can be a powerful instrument for poverty reduction.

* Researchers have devoted special attention to expectancies in the prediction of drinking behavior and alcohol-related problem.

* Most researchers concur that indigenous people prefer the term "family violence" in mainstream society.

(3) Evaluation of Work under Review (present simple tense/ present perfect tense)

* Studies into the effects on bone density are unclear.

* Few studies in the literature deal with the design of an integrated transit network…

* This paper seeks to evaluate the occurrence of polycyclic aromatic hydrocarbons (PAHS) in ambient air particulates.

* This study is useful because it found that there is a strong correlation between public and private sector clients, suggesting that…

* The current study seeks to compare the traditional study practices of English vocabulary in one Chinese university, with a game-based approach.

* As the above summaries indicate, migration research that, at least implicitly, considers knowledge transactions, has been limited in scale and fragmented.

* Notwithstanding these findings, there are still several gaps in the current state

of knowledge regarding the role of vehicle safety in the vehicle purchase process.

* Prior research efforts do not identify the required resources or adjust the resource productivity rates to account for the production impact of different features and different estimators' rationale.

(4) Showing Research Gaps (present simple tense/past simple tense/ present perfect tense)

* Up to now no significant study of air pollution has been carried out.

* The study of the essence of teaching process has made few achievements in the recent 20 years.

* The data available in literature failed to prove that blue quarks could be measurable.

* Nevertheless, these attempts to establish a link between secondary smoke and lung cancer are at present unconvincing.

* No studies/Few studies were included in the same model have been found.

* However, speech recognition is not yet advanced enough to provide people with a reliable listening typewriter.

* Despite the apparent consensus about what to do, there still remains the problem of how cooperation is best achieved.

* Kidney transplantation has been one of the major medical advances of the past 30 years. However, tissue availability remains a major obstacle.

* However, the previously mentioned methods suffer from some limitations mainly concerning the treatment of the vortex wake formation and its interaction with the body.

* Despite the importance of ESCS in developmental biology and their potential impact on tissue replacement therapy, the molecular mechanism underlying ESC self-renewal is poorly understood.

* Although numerous local or global brands of different product categories have been employed to measure brand equity, little information on brand equity within the service industry can be found.

(5) Conclusion as to What Further Study Can Be Done

* Further research is still required with respect to Kriegsmann's model.

* It would seem that there is a need for further research in this area.

* Better mechanical properties could possibly be achieved with further study.

* Based on the literature above, three perspectives will be guiding this article.

* In summary, we sought to replicate and extend a stress or vulnerability model of adolescent alcohol consumption and…

* Although there are previous studies that looked at changes in family-related attitudes in the U.S., the cross-national research is rare.

* To summarize, surprisingly little empirical support has been found so far for depressive deficits in the processing of neutral information.

* This article presents a computational model that aims to solve the optimization problem through a combination of heuristic and analytical approaches.

* With the help of more recent and systematic data at the provincial level, the present study attempts to add to the literature by empirically investigating…

* Although these theories diverge in various ways, there is agreement that emerge between adolescence and young adulthood.

2) Methodology

(1) Providing a General Introduction to the Material/Methods Used and Giving Their Sources

* The impact tests used in this work were a modified version of…

* SSCE glass structures were used in this study to perform…

* All reactions were performed in a 27ml glass reactor…

* Both experiments were performed in a greenhouse so that…

* All cell lines were generated as previously described in…

* The experiments were conducted at a temperature of 0.5.

* The substrate was obtained from the Mushroom Research Center…

* In the majority of the tests, buffers with a pH of B were used in order to…

* Topographical examination was carried out using a 3D stylus instrument.

* The cylindrical lens was obtained from Newport USA and is shown in Fig.3.

(2) Supplying Essential Background Information

* The intercooler was mounted on the top of the engine...

* The concentration of barium decreases towards the edge...

* Similar loads were applied to the front and side of the box...

* The protein was over-expressed and purified as reported previously.

* A revised version of the Structured Clinical Interview 6 was used.

* The size of the Gaussians was adjusted as in... (Krissian et al., 2000)

* A laminar flow element was located downstream of the test section of the wind tunnel...

* The first section of the survey included nine questions measuring fashion opinion leadership on a 7-point Likert scale.

* The questions were adapted from a scale of product-specific opinion leadership developed by Flynn et al. (1996)

* In our implementation we followed Sato et al. (1998) by using a discrete kernel size.

* The centrifuge is a slightly modified commercially available model, the Beckman J6HC.

* Developmental evaluation was carried out using the Bayley Scales of Infant Development (Bayley, 1969)

(3) Justifying Choices Made

* By partitioning the array, all the multipaths could be identified.

* For the sake of simplicity, only a single value was analyzed.

* The LVDTS were unrestrained, so allowing the samples to move freely.

* Zinc oxide was drawn into the laminate with the intention of enhancing delaminations and cracks.

* The advantage of using three-dimensional analysis was that the out-of-plane stress field could be obtained.

* Because FITC was used for both probes, enumeration was carried out using two different slides.

* The method of false nearest neighbours was selected in order to determine the embedding dimension.

* To validate the results from the metroscale model, samples were collected from all groups.

(4) Indicating Where Problems Occurred

* Inevitably, considerable computation was involved.

* Solutions using (q=1) differed slightly from the analytical solutions.

* Only a brief observation was feasible, however, given the number in the sample.

* While the anode layer was slightly thicker than 13um, this was a minor deficit.

* Although centrifugation could not remove all the excess solid drug, the amount remaining was negligible.

* Continuing research will examine a string of dc-dc converters to determine if the predicted efficiencies can be achieved in practice.

3) Results and Discussion

(1) Communicating the value of your research

* The presence of such high levels is a novel finding.

* We identify dramatically different profiles in adult lungs.

* Our results provide compelling evidence that this facilitated infection.

* We have derived exact analytic expressions for the percolation threshold.

* These preliminary results demonstrate the feasibility of using hologram-based RI detectors.

* Our data rule out the possibility that this behavior was a result of neurological abnormal.

* Our study provides the framework for future studies to assess the performance characteristics.

* Our results provide a clear distinction between the functions of the pathway proteins...

* We have made the surprising observation that Bro1- GFP focus accumulation is also pH-dependent.

* The results are expected to be useful in testing realization of the algorithm in computer algebra system and elsewhere.

(2) Application/ Applicability/Implementation

* Our technique can be applied to a wide range of simulation applications.

* It should be possible, therefore, to integrate the HOE onto a microchip.

* This could eventually lead to the identification of novel biomarkers.

* This approach has potential in areas such as fluid density measurement.

* The solution method could be applied without difficulty to irregular-shaped slabs.

* The PARASEX reactor therefore could be used for the realistic testing of a wide range of control algorithms.

* Our results mean that in dipping reservoirs, compositional gradients can now be produced very quickly.

(3) Limitations/ Current and Future Research

* This finding is promising and should be explored with other eukaryotes.

* Our results are encouraging and should be validated in a larger cohort of women.

* However, the neural mechanisms underlying these effects remain to be determined.

* Future work should focus on the efficiency of ligand synthesized in the Long group.

* An important question for future studies is to determine the anti-depressant effects of such drugs.

(4) Explaining What You Have Done to Simplify a Diagram

* I have left a lot of details out, but in any case this should help you to...

* For the sake of simplicity, I have reduced all the numbers to whole numbers.

* For ease of presentation, I have only included essential information.

* This is an extremely simplified view of the situation, but it is enough to illustrate that...

* In reality, this table should also include other factors, but for the sake of simplicity I have just chosen these two key points.

* This is obviously not an exact/accurate picture of the real situation, but it should give you an idea of...

(5) Explaining the Diagram (lines, curves, arrows)

* The horizontal arrows indicate...

* Time is represented by a dotted line.

* There is a slight/gradual/sharp/sudden decrease in...

* As you can see, this wavy curve has a series of peaks and troughs.

* As shown in the chart, the production last month rose significantly...

* As can be seen from the chart, only 10% of the time is taken up with sports activities.

* It is clear/apparent from the table that as incomes increase, people can afford to live more comfortably.

* In this diagram, double circles mean that... whereas black circles mean... dashed lines mean..., and continuous lines mean...

* The figures/statistics show that the total number of visitors to the United States had nearly doubled to 2.7 million people by 2009.

* According to the table/chart/diagram/graph/figures, that downward flow induced by tip vortices limits the growth of the leading-edge vortex.

* The number of...increased suddenly/jumped rapidly/decreased sharply/dropped steeply/fluctuated slowly/go up/go down from...to...

* The table/chart/diagram/graph shows/describes/illustrates that the number of moves between key concepts per 10 t-units correlated most closely with the teachers' marks.

7.3.2 Language Focus

1) Using Proper Language

Compared with the language in an essay, the language used in an oral presentation should be simple, less formal or even colloquial because your aim is to communicate rather than to show off your writing skill and range of vocabulary. Therefore, it is necessary to master some signposting phrases which are used to help guide the audience through a presentation.

2) Saying What Is Coming

* So, let me give you a brief overview...

* In this part of my presentation, I'd like to tell you about...

3) Moving on to the Next Point

* This leads directly to the next part of my talk.

* This now leads us to my next point.

* Let's move on to the next point.

* Let's now turn to the next issue.

4) Talk about (Difficult) Issues

* I think we first need to **identify** the problem.

* We will have to **take care of** this problem now.

* How shall we **cope with** the smog in Beijing?

* Of course we'll have to **clarify** a few points before we start.

* We will have to **deal with** the problem of global warming.

* The question is: Why don't we **tackle** the distribution problems?

* If we don't **solve** this problem now, we'll get into serious trouble soon.

5) Emphasizing Important Points

(1) Using a Verb

* I'd like to **stress** the following points.

* I'd like to **draw** your attention to the latest figures.

* I'd like to **emphasize** that point.

(2) Using "What"

* **What** is really important is how much we are prepared to invest.

* **What** we should do is talk about intercultural problems.

(3) Using Rhetorical Questions

* So, just how good are the results?

* So where will we go?

* Why do I say that? Because...

(4) Adverb + Adjective Construction

* I think this fact is **extremely important**.

* It would be **completely wrong** to change our strategy at this point.

* We compared the two offers and found the first one **totally unacceptable**.

6) Referring to Other Points

* There are a few problems **regarding** the quality.

* **With respect/regard** to price, we need more details.

* **According to** the survey, our customers are unhappy with this product.

* I'd like to mention some critical points **in connection with/concerning** payment.

7) Adding Ideas

* **As well as that**, we can offer excellent conditions.

* **Apart from** being too expensive, this model is also too big.

* To increase sales, we need a new strategy **plus** more people.

* **In addition to** this, I'd like to say that our new energy business is going very well.

* **Moreover/Furthermore**, there are other interesting facts we should take a look at.

In addition to the signposting phrases above, you should also note the use of voice and body language. The following are suggestions for delivering your oral presentation:

(1) Speak loudly, slowly and clearly, especially in terms of key words and important points. Do not rush! Speaking fast might make it harder for other people to understand you.

(2) Vary your voice quality. If you always use the same volume and pitch, you will

doze off your audience. Use a higher pitch and volume when you begin a new point.

(3) Vary your speed. Speak with a particularly slow and deliberate voice when you emphasize key points.

(4) Use pauses. Do not be afraid of short periods of silence when you want to draw attention to a particular point. Silence can be articulate. Leave a long pause to give your audience a chance to think and let the key point sink in.

(5) Use body language. Do not look at your notes or your computer screen all the time. Do not stare, or look blankly into people's eyes. Hold your head up, look around and make eye contact with your audience. Do not speak motionlessly. Move around the room and gesture with hands and arms to project a feeling of energy and excitement, to emphasize your points, and to engage your audience.

Reflections and Practice (2)

Prepare the main part of a presentation using phrases from this unit. Use the checklist to help.

* Briefly state your topic again.
* Explain your objectives.
* Signal the beginning of each part.
* Talk about your topic.
* Signal the end of each part.
* Highlight the main points.
* Outline the main ideas in bullet-point form.
* Tell listeners you've reached the end of the main part.

7.4 Summary and Interaction with Audience

Starter:

Look at these sentences from the presentation and put them in the correct category in the table below (Grussendorf, 2007: 43).

Unit 7 Preparing Oral Presentation

a. I'll just run through the three different options...

b. We'd suggest...

c. Now I'll be happy to answer any questions you may have.

d. We therefore recommend that we...

e. Before I stop, let me go through my main points again.

f. Well, this brings me to the end of my presentation.

Conclusion of a Presentation
Signaling the end of the presentation:
Summarizing the main points:
Recommending or suggesting something:
Inviting questions:

Now add these phrases to the table above

g. Thank you all for listening.

h. In my opinion, we should...

i. OK, I think that's everything I wanted to say...

j. To sum up then, we...

k. We just have time for a few questions.

l. Are there any questions?

m. I'd like to run through my main points again...

n. As a final point, I'd like to...

o. I'm now nearing the end of my talk...

p. Just to summarize the main points of my talk...

q. What I'd like to suggest is...

1) Structure Focus for Summary

(1) Signaling the End of the Presentation

* Before I stop/ finish, let me just say...

* To close my speech, I'll show you the last slide.

* That's all for my presentation. Thank you very much.

* To end my presentation, I would like to present you the last slide.

* Well, that brings me to the end of my presentation. This last slide is a brief summary of what I have talked about.

(2) Summarizing the Main Points and Indicating the Conclusion

* I'll briefly summarize the main issues.

* To sum up.../ Briefly.../In summary... /In conclusion...

* Let me conclude my speech with the following words.

* In conclusion, I'd like to emphasize the following points.

* To conclude, I'd like to summarize my talk by making four points.

* Finally, as a summary statement, I would like to sum up the major points I have made.

* To close my speech, I would like to sum up the major points I have already made.

* To sum up, it has been shown that listening to classical music will help us sharpen up our inspiration.

* In summary, it can be concluded that the sea water of the whole world contains 100 trillion tons of bromine.

* Based on detailed factual observations and discussions, it is concluded that dinosaurs walked slowly at a speed of 3.6 km per hour or more.

* Summarizing the main points discussed here, we can conclude that the so-called extrasensory perception can be accounted for scientifically.

* Based on the above detailed observations, we naturally come to the conclusion that the leaves of those plants which were deprived of the amount of magnesium necessary for forming chlorophyll will turn yellow.

(3) Expressing Hopes and Thanks

* I would be glad if this is of any help to those concerned.

* Thank you very much for this opportunity/ your attention /listening.

* I hope this conference will make a significant contribution to its speedy realization.

* I am hopeful that the conference will end with fruitful outcomes and pave ways for further discussions as well as similar arrangements in the near future.

* At the very end of my presentation, let me say a few words of thanks to the people who gave me valuable suggestions in organizing my presentation.

* We look forward to working closely with NGOS and other civil society organizations in reducing poverty and improving living standards of the people...

* We believe, with joint efforts of different countries, renewable energy will surely develop faster and better and will play promotional role in global sustainable development.

* Finally, Mr. Chairman, I would like to take the opportunity to thank the Chinese government, especially, the Yunnan University, for sponsoring and organizing this conference and the excellent arrangements made.

* In concluding these brief introductory remarks, we wish to express our gratitude to all the participants in this conference for contributing and giving us an invaluable opportunity to create a lively and enthusiastic research groups.

* Without taking any longer time of the conference, I would like to express my sincere appreciation once again to the host of this conference which provides me wonderful opportunities to exchange views and comments on ways to further strengthen trade and economic cooperation between ASEAN and China.

2) Language Focus for Summary

In order to write effective conclusions, you may refer to the following tips:

(1) Using Questions

* After all, isn't that why we're here?

* Let me just finish with a question: If we don't do it, won't somebody else?

(2) Quoting a Well-known Person

* As...once said,...

* To quote a well-known environmentalist,...

* To put it in the words of...,...

(3) Referring back to the Beginning

* Remember what I said at the beginning of my talk today? Well,...

* Let me just go back to the story I told you earlier. Remember,...

(4) Calling the Audience to Action

* So that's the plan. Now let's go and put it into practice!

* So now it's your turn.

* Now let's make a real effort to achieve this goal!

Reflections and Practice (3)

Follow the checklist to practise making conclusions. Try to use words and phrases from the unit.

* Signal the end of your talk.
* Summarize the key points.
* Highlight one important point.
* Explain the significance.
* Make your final statement.

Once you finish your talk you may invite questions from your audience if time is allowed. There are some tips for dealing with questions, asking polite questions, dealing with interruptions and reforming questions.

3) Structure Focus for Interaction with Audience

(1) Announcing the Beginning of the Question and Answer Session

* We'll proceed into the question and answer period.

* It's time for Q&A. Will you raise a hand to ask a question?

* I would like to get some comments or questions from the panel.

* Now Dr. Cage seems ready to answer your questions. Any questions?

Unit 7 Preparing Oral Presentation

* Now, ladies and gentlemen, we would like to invite questions or comments.

* You are requested to put forward your frank opinions and views concerning my speech.

* We do have time for a couple of questions before wrap-up, so let's go right here first.

* Now there is an opportunity for any questions, comments, or concerns you may have for the speakers.

* Thank you very much for your attention. Now we will proceed to a question and answer session.

* We have a 10-minute question and answer session: Is there any person who would like to ask a question?

* I'd like to open it up now and have a question and answer session and a round-table discussion if we could. If you could, please speak into the microphone.

* We have only one minute left for this session. We would like to have one question. And this is the last question. Is there any person who still wants to ask a question?

(2) Raising Questions

* Let me ask a question about it.

* May I trouble you with a question?

* I was wondering if I could ask some questions.

* Could you be more specific in your explanation?

* I'd like to ask you the following questions to have a better look into the subject.

* Let me ask you a couple of questions concerning an early part of your lecture.

* Can you enlarge on your opinion of the writer's influence on the literary world?

* You have so far told us about the positive aspects of the theory. Would you like to give us an example of a negative aspect if any.

* Interesting points have been made. Then, would you elaborate a little more on the first two points?

* Could you explain the process of synthesizing those chemicals in your experimental study?

* First of all, I enjoyed your talk very much. Could you elaborate on the feasibility of the plan to develop a simultaneous translating device?

(3) Commenting on the Question and Responding to the Questioner

* I appreciate that question.

* I'm glad this question has been brought up.

* I'd be delighted to answer your question.

* I'll try to answer this question very briefly.

* I have to admit that you are right in a sense.

* I can only provide a partial answer to that question.

* This is a very good/ big/hard/ interesting question.

* The question I got here is a very insightful one. I am happy to answer it.

* The question you raised right now is a very challenging one, but I will try.

* Actually by using my theory I think I cannot solve the problem you posed right now.

* Thank you for that question. This is a challenging question, and I'm afraid I can only provide a partial answer to it. Anyway I'll try my best to answer it.

* You just asked me a question which is hard for me to answer quickly, I will leave it open for my next presentation. Do you have any further comments?

(4) Making Questioner to Repeat the Questions

* Could you go over that again?

* I'm not sure what you're getting at.

* Pardon, I couldn't hear what you said.

* I beg your pardon. I didn't catch what you said/ that.

* I am not quite sure what your question is.

* I didn't quite get the last point of your question.

* If I understand you correctly, you are saying/asking...

* Are you referring to the significance of the difference?

* Are you suggesting that the temperature might have affected the results?

* I don't quite understand your question. Would you be more specific?

* I'm sorry I forgot your first question. Would you be so kind as to repeat it?

4) Language Focus for Interaction with Audience

(1) Dealing with Questions

<u>Asking for clarification</u>

* I'm sorry. Could you repeat your question, please?

* I'm afraid I didn't quite catch that.

* I'm afraid I don't quite understand your question.

<u>Avoiding giving an answer</u>

* If you don't mind, I'd prefer not to discuss that today.

* Perhaps we could deal with this after the presentation/ at some other time.

* I'm afraid that's not really what we are here to discuss today.

* When doing this, make sure that your tone of voice is friendly and your reply is polite.

<u>Admitting you don't know the answer or responding to challenging questions.</u>

* The answer to this question needs further study.

* I would like to give this pointed question an elegant answer.

* Perhaps my colleague Dr. Emery here has some better ideas.

* I think that question could be better answered by Dr. Liu than by me.

* Sorry, that's not my field. But I'm sure... could answer your question.

* I'm afraid I'm not in a position to answer that. Perhaps... could help.

* I wish I could answer your question, but ultimately I have no good answer.

* I'm afraid I don't know the answer to your question, but I'll try to find out for you.

* I'm not sure that I can answer your question. What I'm going to say is not quite an answer to your question.

* Prof. Li would be a better person to answer your question since he has done a lot of work in this field.

* Perhaps in another year or so we'll be able to answer that question because

the studies are now in progress.

* The only answer I can give at present is to wait a few more years at which time something better might ultimately come out of all our efforts.

(2) Asking Polite Questions

<u>Direct or impolite questions</u>

* What's the project status?

* When do you plan to investigate into this?

<u>Less direct or more polite questions</u>

* Do you mind if I ask what the project status is?

* Could you tell me when you plan to investigate into this?

(3) Dealing with Interruptions

* If you don't mind, I'll deal with this question later in my presentation.

* Can we get back to that a bit later?

* Would you mind waiting with your questions until the question and answer session at the end?

After answering questions, especially those that require a longer answer, it is sometimes necessary to remind the audience what you were talking about before the interruption.

* Before we continue, let me briefly summarize the points we were discussing.

* So, back to what I was saying about…

(4) Asking a Specific Question, or Questions for Specific or Additional Information

* You mentioned very briefly that you used two experiments that were the same, would you please elaborate on that point?

* Would you be so kind as to give me more information about the method of your experiment?

* Would you tell me the reason why you set such a high temperature?

* Mr. Smith, what do you refer to by getting a peak value?

* I don't quite understand what you really mean by saying "…" Can you explain it again?

* I'm still confused about the relationship between the temperature and the epidemic. Could you talk about that again?

* I'm very keen on what you say about the growing process of a cell. Could you tell me exactly how long it would take a cell of the microorganism to grow into a full body?

* I'm very interested in hearing your presentation today on cigarette smoking and Parkinson's disease. Would you please say a few more words about the tentative assumption, particularly at its preliminary stage?

(5) Reforming Questions

It is sometimes necessary to reformulate a question (say it in another way) before answering it. This not only gives you time to think, but also allows you to make sure you have understood the question, as the following expressions show (Grussendorf, 2007: 56):

* I see. So, what you are asking is...

* If I understand you correctly, you want to know...

* OK, let me just repeat your question so everybody can hear it.

* If I could just rephrase your question...

The question is:	You reformulate to make it:	By:
Negative Isn't there a better solution?	Positive What would be a better solution?	Leaving out negative words such as *no, never, none*
Aggressive Do you honestly believe we can get the contact?	Neutral You're asking whether I think it is possible to get the contact.	Avoiding words which sound aggressive or have a negative meaning such as *honestly, really, disaster*

Reflections and Practice (4)

Practise the phrases from this unit using the checklist.

<u>Checklist for questions</u>

* Listen carefully.

* Make sure you have understood the question correctly.

* Reformulate the question in your own words.

* If you want to postpone the question, say why politely.

* If you don't know the answer, say so and offer to find out.

* Answer irrelevant questions politely but briefly.

* Check whether the questioner is satisfied with your answer.

7.5 Using Visual Aids

Starter: Do you know the English names of these media and tools used in presentations? (Grussendorf, 2007: 23)

The most common visual aids include PPTs, handouts and white/black boards. PPTs are the easiest and most reliable form of visual aids. But do not read word-for-word from your PPT. When producing your PPT (蔡基刚, 2012: 283),

a. reduce the major points in the lecture to words and phrases. Do not put a complete sentence on the slides unless you use direct quotations;

b. use bold typeface, and a reasonable size (e.g. 38 point text and 42~50 point titles) so that the audience can see your words clearly;

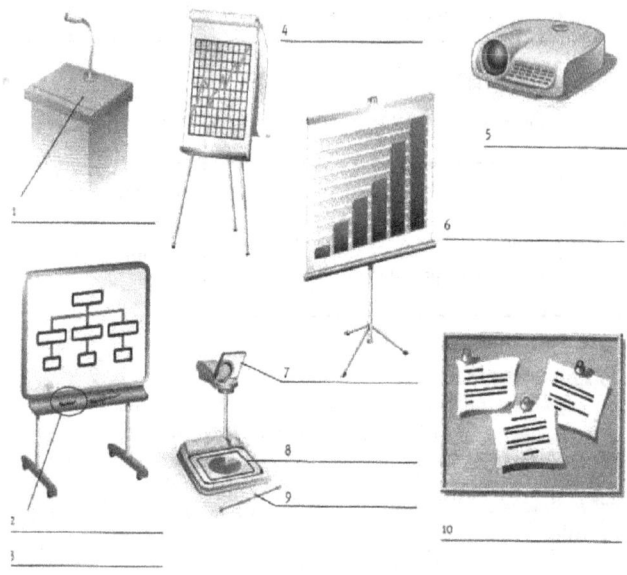

c. use double space and give your audience time to take notes when they read watch slide. A wise speaker rarely puts more than twelve words on a slide;

d. use colors, pictures and graphs which can make your PPTs more interesting and effective. But do not overcrowd with too much detail.

e. believe simplicity is the best aesthetic tactic. Your audience has very little time to absorb what is on your slide. Most of people tend to spend more time producing PowerPoint graphics than on the actual talk. But if your talk is poor, no amount of fancy graphics will save it!

1) Presenting the visual

When presenting text on overheads or PowerPoint slides, it is a good idea to use the *rule of six* which means a maximum of six lines per slide and a maximum of six words per line. The following tips may guide you toward a better slide.

(1) Choose the shortest forms possible (王慧莉, 2015: 64-65)

necessary	needed
regarding	on
however	but
furthermore	also
consequently	so
as soon as possible	ASAP
to be continued	tbc.
for example	e.g.
that is to say	i.e.
information	info
against	vs
research and development	R&D
10,000	10k

wordy pattern	Make a comparison between X and Y.
simple pattern	Compare X and Y.

wordy pattern	There is a possibility that X will fail.
simple pattern	X may fail.

wordy pattern	The activity of testing is a laborious process.
simple pattern	Testing is laborious.

(2) Reduce duplication between the text of your slide and the script of your presentation

a. (Grussendorf, 2007: 27)

> SAIC Group 2007
> • subsidiaries: 55
> • joint ventures: 63
> • employees: 60,000
> • vehicles: 800,000
> • sales: $12bn

b.

> 2007-Car Production of SAIC in China
> • has 55 subsidiaries and 63 joint ventures
> • employs more than 60,000 people
> • produces about 800,000 vehicles
> • generates sales of $12 billion

(3) Cut brackets containing text (examples, definitions or statistics) (王慧莉, 2015: 67)

Original slide	alternative energy (solar, wind, nuclear, etc.)
Edited slide	alternative energy
Script	Today we are going to explore such alternative energies as solar energy, wind energy and even nuclear energy.

Unit 7 Preparing Oral Presentation

Original slide	ISO (International Organization for Standardization) approval
Edited slide	ISO approval
Script	Our equipment has been approved by the International Organization for Standardization.

Question: What is important when presenting visuals? Which opinion do you agree with?

2) Explaining the visual

Sometimes it is necessary to explain a very complicated visual and it is always necessary to point out the most important information.

(1) Explaining a Visual

* First, let me quickly explain the graph.

* Let's now look at the next slide which shows…

* The key in the bottom left-handed corner shows you…

* You can see that different colors have been used to indicate…

(2) Highlighting Information

* What I'd like to point out here is…

* I think you'll be surprised to see…

* I'd like you to focus your attention on…

* Let's look more closely at…

* I'd like to start by drawing your attention to…

(3) Talking about Trends

* Petrol prices rose again in May.

* The number has risen to 2.6 million.

* The oil industry raised prices last year.

* There was a sudden increase in prices.

* In August, we notice a moderate fall.

* This was followed by a gradual decline.

* Sales increased slightly in summer.

* Over the past two years the number has dropped significantly.

Reflections and Practice (5)

Prepare bullet charts based on your own data. Find an effective headline for each bullet chart and present them to a partner. Use the checklist to help.

Checklist for visuals

* Prepare each visual carefully and separately.

* Check whether the visual really shows what you are saying.

* Make sure your audience can read the visual (font size and colors).

* Find effective headlines.

* Keep design and content simple.

* Use bullet charts for text.

* Reduce text to a minimum.

* Always prepare audience for visuals.

* Present information clearly and logically.

* Remember the rule of six.

Checklist for using graphs and charts

* Make your visual as clear and easy to understand as possible.

* Start by telling your audience what the graph/chart illustrates.

* Highlighting the key points.

* Say why these points are important (and explain the cause or effect).

* Use different verbs to express movement/development.

* Use the same key words and phrases you used on your bullet charts.

Bibliography

［1］蔡基刚.学术英语［M］.北京：外语教学与研究出版社,2012.

［2］陈宏薇.汉英翻译基础［M］.上海：上海外语教育出版社,1998.

［3］陈文伯.译艺——英汉汉英双向笔译［M］.北京：世界知识出版社,2004.

［4］陈新仁.英语学术论文写作实用教程［M］.苏州：苏州大学出版社,2012.

［5］程爱民,祁寿华.英语学术论文写作纲要［M］.上海：上海外语教育出版社,2005.

［6］高霄.学术英语论文写作［M］.北京：外语教学与研究出版社,2015.

［7］龚杰.英语学术论文高级写作技巧和发表指南［M］.成都：四川大学出版社,2017.

［8］郭继荣.学术论文写作与发表［M］.西安：西安交通大学出版社,2012.

［9］胡庚申.文献阅读与翻译［M］.北京：高等教育出版社,2003.

［10］胡庚申.英语论文写作与国际发表［M］.北京：外语教学与研究出版社,2014.

［11］黄国文,葛达西,张美芳.英语学术论文写作［M］.重庆：重庆大学出版社,2014.

［12］何广湘,杨索,靳海波.气升式环流反应器的研究进展［J］.化学工业与工程,2008,1.

［13］姜秋霞.研究生英语学术论文写作基础［M］.上海：复旦大学出版社,2016.

［14］李达,李玉成,李春艳.SCI论文写作解析［M］.北京：清华大学出

版社, 2012.

［15］李桂荣. 英语学术期刊论文写作原理与实务（经管卷）［M］. 天津：南开大学出版社, 2008.

［16］李向武. 英语学术论文写作教程［M］. 成都：西南交通大学出版社, 2014.

［17］李芝. 英语学术论文写作教程［M］. 北京：中国人民大学出版社, 2017.

［18］林煌天. 中国翻译词典［M］. 武汉：湖北教育出版社, 1997.

［19］刘承宇, Patton, M.D. 学术英语写作教程［M］. 北京：中国人民大学出版社, 2015.

［20］刘洊波. 英语学术论文写作［M］. 北京：高等教育出版社, 2004.

［21］刘宓庆. 新编汉英对比与翻译［M］. 北京：中国对外翻译出版公司, 2006.

［22］刘宇红. 实用英语学术论文写作［M］. 北京：对外经贸大学出版社, 2014.

［23］刘振聪, 修月祯. 英语学术论文写作［M］. 北京：中国人民大学出版社, 2013.

［24］马莉. 英语学术论文写作及语体风格［M］. 北京：北京大学出版社, 2011.

［25］彭金定, 赵培玲. 学术论文写作实用指南［M］. 长沙：中南大学出版社, 2015.

［26］申雨平, 等. 实用汉英翻译教程［M］. 北京：外语教学与研究出版社, 2002.

［27］王慧莉, 等. 国际学术会议英语［M］. 北京：中国人民大学出版社, 2015.

［28］文斌. 英语专业学术论文写作教程［M］. 武汉：华中科技大学出版社, 2010.

［29］吴江梅, 黄佩娟. 英语科技论文写作［M］. 北京：中国人民大学出版社, 2013.

［30］谢小苑. 科技英语翻译［M］. 北京：国防工业出版社, 2015.

［31］徐喜文. 英语学术论文写作导读：信度与权威［M］. 武汉：华中科技大学出版社, 2011.

［32］张建, 陈赟. SCI/EI 学术论文写作与发表攻略［M］. 北京：机械工业出版社, 2018.

［33］张培基, 等. 英汉翻译教程［M］. 上海：上海外语教育出版社, 1986.

［34］周开鑫. 英语专业学生学术论文写作手册［M］. 北京：外语教学与研究出版社, 2006.

［35］周南润, 黄鹏, 刘晔, 等. 两步量子安全直接通信协议的信息论分析［J］. 量子光学学报, 2008, 4.

［36］Bruce, I. Academic Writing and Genre: A Systematic Analysis［M］. London: Bloomsbury Academic, 2010.

［37］CoyleWilliam, Law Joe. Research Paper［M］. 16th ed. 北京：北京语言大学出版社, 2015.

［38］Ebrahimi, S. etc.（2018）. California End-use Electrification Impacts on Carbon Neutrality and Clean Air［J］. Applied Energy, 213.

［39］Gastel, B. & Robert A. D. 科技论文写作与发表教程.［M］. 曾剑芬, 译. 6th ed. 北京：电子工业出版社, 2018.

［40］Grussendorf, Marion. English for Presentations［M］. Oxford: Oxford University Press, 2007.

［41］John Sinclair. Collins Cobuild English-Chinese Dictionary［A］. 上海：上海译文出版社, 2002.

［42］Munday, J. Introducing Translation Studies［M］. London & New York: Routledge, 2001.

［43］Nida, E. A. Language and Culture Contexts in Translating［M］. Shanghai: Shanghai Foreign Language Education Press, 2001.

［44］Slade, C., Robert P. Handbook for Writing Research Papers, Reports, and Theses［M］. 北京：外语教学与研究出版社, 2011.

[45] Taylor, N. Academic Writing: A Handbook for International Students [M]. London: Routledge, 2014.

[46] Winkler, Anthony C., McCuen-Metherell. Writing the Research Paper: A Handbook [M]. 北京：北京大学出版社, 2017.